THE ALTERNATIVE HOLIDAY GUIDE TO

The Waterways of Britain and Europe

by

Eric and Ruth Bailey

ASHFORD

Southampton

Published by Ashford
            1 Church Road,
            Shedfield,
            Hampshire
            SO3 2HW

British Library Cataloguing in Publication Data

Bailey, Eric
   The alternative holiday guide to the waterways of Britain and Europe.
   1. Europe. Inland waterways. Description & travel
   I. Title II. Bailey, Ruth
   914′.04558

   ISBN 1–85253–188–6

Printed by Hartnolls Ltd, Bodmin, Cornwall, England

Phototypeset in 10/11½ Century by Input Typesetting Ltd, London

Contents

CONTENTS

CONTENTS

Photographs

Maps

Acknowledgements

The authors and publisher would like to thank the following for their invaluable assistance during the researching of this book: Associated Leisure Hotels; Association Régionale pour le Développement du Tourisme Fluviale Nord-Pas de Calais; Belgian Tourist Office; Blakes Holidays; Bridgewater Boats; British Waterways; Charter Cruising Company; Copthorne Hotels; Egerton Narrow Boats; Erincurrach Cruising; Tom Garrod; Green Waterway Holidays; Hoseasons Holidays; Irish Tourist Board; KLM Royal Dutch Airlines; Netherlands Board of Tourism; Netherlands Railways; Northern Ireland Tourist Board; P & O Ferries; Snaygill Boats; Yachting Sirius BV – to say nothing of all the boaters, gongoozlers, British Waterways staff, Inland Waterways Association members and other waterway users who helped to make the task such a delightful one.

The majority of the photographs in this book were taken by the authors and by Peter Garrod. Others were provided by Blakes Holidays, Bradford Tourism Department, Hoseasons Holidays, Irish Tourist Board, Manchester City Council, UK Waterway Holidays and Wigan Pier.

INTRODUCTION

Canal art

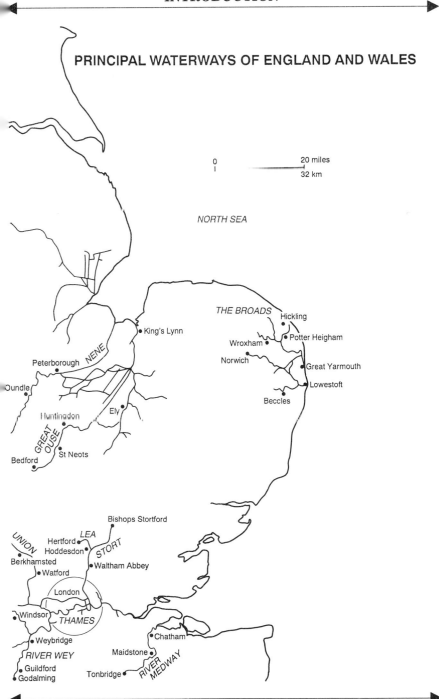

PRINCIPAL WATERWAYS OF ENGLAND AND WALES

0   20 miles
32 km

NORTH SEA

THE BROADS   Hickling

King's Lynn

Wroxham   Potter Heigham

Peterborough   *NENE*   Norwich

Great Yarmouth

Oundle   Lowestoft

Huntingdon   Ely   Beccles

GREAT OUSE

Bedford   St Neots

Bishops Stortford

UNION   *LEA*   Hertford

Hoddesdon   *STORT*

Berkhamsted   Waltham Abbey

Watford

London

Windsor   *THAMES*

Weybridge   Chatham

RIVER WEY   Maidstone

Guildford   Tonbridge   *RIVER MEDWAY*

Godalming

Most waterways in Britain, if not abroad, are already well documented for the amateur navigator, so we have set out in *The Alternative Holiday Guide to The Waterways of Britain and Europe* to capture the spirit of a holiday afloat rather than providing a bridge-by-bridge or lock-by-lock account of what each canal and river has to offer. The Continent and the British Isles together provide thousands of miles of navigable waterways for people to enjoy in their leisure time – from Britain's narrow canals and the Broads of England and Holland, to the rivers and lakes of Scotland and Ireland, and the busy liquid highways of France and Belgium – and in this book we present a selection of those which in our view offer some of the best holiday cruising opportunities.

We have restricted our coverage of continental waterways to those in France, Belgium and Holland because they provide the widest choice of comparatively easy waters to navigate with no restricting formalities for skippers of hire craft. In Germany, for example, you need a certificate of competence to take charge of a boat. Sweden has an excellent inland waterway system, very similar to that in England – indeed the English canal engineer Thomas Telford had a hand in its development – but we feel Sweden is out of reach, both in terms of distance and expense, for the average holiday boater.

The guide is directed mainly at first-time hirers wondering whether an inland boating holiday is right for them, but those who are seeking to expand their experience on different waters, perhaps in different craft and lands may also find it useful. The chapters are interspersed, here and there, with 'Waterludes' in which we introduce a number of waterway personalities, who enthusiastically express their own experiences of inland boating. They include some of the professionals whose work helps provide a really enjoyable, truly *alternative* holiday for many thousands of people.

Who Uses the Waterways?

While taking the boater's viewpoint, we have taken account of the wide range of interests pursued by other waterway users – the anglers, towpath walkers, ornithologists, botanists, wildlife watchers, history buffs, photographers and industrial archaeologists. Each of these activities is, of course, available to the holidaymaker afloat, so your trip can be several holidays in one, with the pleasure of meeting people with similar interests, calling at waterside pubs and generally enjoying the camaraderie of the cut.

The people who cruise the waterways come from countless walks of life and every age group. With the possible exception, unless they are very well disciplined, of toddlers from about 18 months to three years old, a waterways holiday can be enjoyed by everyone. At the other end of the scale, we have known a one-legged nonagenarian to sit happily in the bow of her schoolmaster son's narrow boat during annual summer holidays of several weeks' duration.

Inland waterways can be enjoyed by the gregarious – parties of young and not so young people who like to live it up at night in quayside discos – and by the loners, those who like to equip themselves with a 12 ft (3.6 m) dinghy, a 6 ft (1.8 m) tent, a sleeping bag and a spirit stove and give themselves up to peace, solitude and nature for a week or two.

Voyage of Discovery

Discovering the tranquil 'other world' – the navigable waterway that hides behind high-rise buildings, alongside a railway line, or beneath a frenzied motorway, *and* through some of the loveliest countryside you'll find anywhere – provides constant surprises.

While the public swarms in and out of Manchester's Piccadilly railway station, a boat may be placidly negotiating a lock 300 yds (270 m) away. Many people who live or work in the city have never noticed the waterborne leisure traffic that moves below street level – though the 1988 Inland Waterways Rally at Castlefields has done much to put the network on the map.

How many motorists zipping hither and thither at Birmingham's Spaghetti Junction realise that a narrow boat may be chugging contentedly along beneath them at four miles an hour? Some of them wouldn't care, of course, but for those bitten by the canal bug it becomes second nature to look out for 'secret' waterways.

In Paris probably few of those exercising their poodles along the Boulevard Richard Lenoir realise that beneath their very feet a *pénichette* may be pushing its way through a mile-long tunnel on its way to the Bassin Villette, where the attractive Canal de l'Ourcq begins a 67-mile (107 km) journey to Port aux Perches, following the River Marne for much of the way.

A New Age Dawns

Two hundred years ago inland waterways were regarded as revolutionary a form of transport as Concorde is today. They enabled new industries to flourish by providing easy access to raw materials and opening up markets in faraway places. Rural areas found new outlets for their produce. People were able to move beyond the confines of their birthplace. Prices tumbled, trade increased, towns grew. The Industrial Age had dawned.

For most people it meant a lifetime of sweat and toil, spending long hours in places dark, noisome, hot and smoky. For those actually working on the canals, of Britain especially – the gypsy-like boat families who spent their lives entirely afloat – at least the air was sometimes clean. But they still worked and lived under appalling conditions, in cramped and dirty surroundings; their health threatened, their children – many children – uneducated.

The railways changed all that. They brought a faster, even cheaper transportation system into use – and the canals of Britain went into decline, silting up through lack of use and maintenance. It was a different story on the Continent where the waterways, wide and deep, have always been regarded as lifelines in the chain of production and consumption. There, commercial use of the system continues to flourish, although leisure boating is also now expanding.

The waterways of Britain would have become a lost heritage had it not been for those who recognised their leisure potential. Successive governments failed to provide the necessary finance to maintain them properly when commercial canal carrying dwindled almost to nothing, despite the fact that the amount of fuel used to carry goods by water is infinitesimal compared with that used by road transport. It was the crusading spirit of organisations such as the Inland Waterways Association, set up after World War II, and its volunteer mudlarks who physically restored locks and navigations – and still do – that has enabled thousands of people to enjoy the waterways in their leisure time.

May they long continue to provide as much interest and delight for others as they have for us.

PLANNING AND PREPARATION

Canalside shops provide a range of services

Choosing a Waterway

Once you have made the decision to take a waterways holiday, you are faced with the question of where to go. Here, you are thoroughly spoilt for choice. A number of factors may influence your decision.

Do you mind driving a long distance to reach a particular region that appeals to you? Would you prefer to hire from a company within, say, a 50-mile radius of your home? How about a holiday on the French canals, or elsewhere in Europe? Can you spare more than a fortnight to explore the entire Avon Ring, or just a few days for the lovely Stratford-upon-Avon Canal which forms part of the Avon Ring?

If you have a particular interest – birdwatching, say, or industrial archaeology – it will be worth while, and no doubt enjoyable, to do some research to find the most suitable locations. Otherwise, just choose a region and follow your nose. There will be plenty to enjoy.

Those interested in **canal history** may choose a route which includes a museum. Small ones exist in many parts of the system, and there are major ones, like the world's largest collection of canal craft afloat, at Ellesmere Port, Cheshire, and the long-established Inland Waterways Museum at Stoke Bruerne, Northamptonshire, which gives an insight into the way of life of the boat families working for the carrying companies of the eighteenth and nineteenth centuries. To understand something of the economics and engineering of building the canals, a visit to the National Waterways Museum opened in Gloucester in 1988 by the Prince of Wales is worth while.

Canal bridges of various styles, the different types of paddles, the locks themselves, some in flights and staircases, hold a fascination for some, and almost everyone going through a tunnel for the first time will find it an unforgettable and slightly scary experience. Crossing an aqueduct can be thrilling, too, especially if it is the spectacular Pontcysyllte on the Llangollen Canal, standing 120 ft (40 m) over the Dee Valley in Wales.

Historic small towns and villages provide added interest along the waterways of Britain, France, Holland and Belgium. Anyone who enjoys forgetting the clock, pottering around in craft shops or old churches, seeking out local foods and the best places to quench a thirst, will be happy on a boating holiday.

Many navigations provide peace and quiet, but that isn't everybody's idea of a memorable holiday. To be sure of evening entertainment, you can cruise through Leeds, Birmingham, Chester, Gloucester, Worcester, Manchester, Warwick, Northampton, Peterborough,

Bath, Oxford, Watford, Stratford-upon-Avon, Milton Keynes, and countless other towns and cities – not forgetting London. Some people, especially knowing visitors from abroad, hire a boat from an operator within 20 miles of London, then cruise along the Grand Union Canal to moor for a few days in the capital. They use the boat as a self-catering base while they do the 'touristy' thing. It costs a lot less than a hotel. Many European cities also have waterways running through them.

Planning a boating holiday is almost as much fun as the event itself, and it is wise to get as much information about suitable cruising areas, and types of craft as early as possible. For a start, you'll get a broad picture of where you can go and what boats are available in both Britain and mainland Europe by looking at the brochures published by Blakes Holidays, Boat Enquiries, Hoseasons Holidays and UK Waterway Holidays. You will also find boating holidays advertised in such publications as *Canal & Riverboat*, *Waterways World* and *Motor Boat and Yachting*. A selection of boatyard and hire company addresses is given at the end of each chapter in this book.

Choosing Your Craft

Hiring a boat

Having a rough idea of where you're going, you can now start musing about what sort of boat you will need. For a number of reasons it is best to hire rather than buy a boat for your first cruising experience. The more boats you hire the easier it is to identify exactly what you want if and when you have the wherewithal to buy your own. Hiring also has the advantage that you can choose a different route each holiday or break you take. Delightful though it is to own a boat, unless it is small enough to trail behind a car, it takes time to get from your home mooring to a waterway you have never cruised before. Furthermore, there is the cost of a permanent mooring, insurance, licence, maintenance, and a dozen etceteras to be taken into account.

Narrow boats

On English and Welsh canals most of the hire craft are brightly painted narrow boats, their steel hulls built more or less to the traditional designs of the old commercial carrying boats – though purists may dispute this. The original narrow boat, up to 72 ft (24 m) long and no more than 6 ft 10 in (2.3 m) in beam, was designed to negotiate the locks and tunnels of narrow-gauge canals built in the early days of the Industrial Revolution. They are ideal for leisure use because in general they have full headroom, plenty of room for preparing meals, generous storage space, safe exterior seating and large windows so that the galley slave need not miss anything.

Wider boats

On rivers – such as the Thames – and wide-gauge waterways, like the Leeds and Liverpool Canal which crosses the Pennines in Northern England, you will find wider beam cruisers and converted barges. On large, open stretches of water, such as Lough Erne in Co. Fermanagh, Northern Ireland, and on Scotland's Caledonian Canal, there will be powerfully engined craft designed for coastal work and equipped with such navigational aids as compasses and depth sounders. Roomy boats with a wide beam and shallow draft have been designed for England's Norfolk Broads and those in northern Holland. These can be tricky to handle if the wind gets up. In France you'll find the ubiquitous *pénichette*, evolved like the English narrow boat from traditional working boats.

Hotel boats

If you don't want the responsibility of handling a boat yourself, then a hotel boat might be more suitable. These are to be found on many waterways in Britain and on the Continent. Standards of accommodation range from modest to outrageously de luxe. On English and Welsh waterways you are likely to find a pair of narrow boats operating as they did in the past – a diesel-powered boat towing an engineless *butty*. One boat will be divided into sleeping quarters – often quite delightful little cabins; the other will have a lounge and dining saloon. Passengers can be as lazy or as active as they like, sunbathing on the roof, strolling on the towpath, or joining in the work of negotiating locks as they choose. At the other end of the scale, on the French canals for instance, there are the big barge conversions, all silk and satin, and one, at least, with a heated swimming pool. Right across the board, the standards of cuisine are surprisingly high.

Hire periods

Many British boat operators hold open days before the season gets under way when members of the public are encouraged to visit their yards and examine their boats. Keep an eye on the boating press to find out the dates. Or you can phone likely boatyards and ask if you may take a look at their fleet. They won't mind, as long as you don't turn up on a Saturday morning when boats are coming and going at the start of a new hire period. After all, it's only practical to take a look at what is available, and to find out what equipment is provided.

What to Look For

Study brochures carefully, or question the operators closely if you meet them personally, to find out about such things as hire periods – some companies will hire from midweek to midweek, which may be more convenient for some people – and the rates charged at different times of the season – they tend to be higher during school holidays. Some operators will hire out craft in winter, and this can be a great time for cruising in these days of centrally heated boats. Yours will probably be the only vessel for miles, and there is something magical about cruising a still, silent waterway on a white-frost morning. Canals can freeze over in very harsh weather, but it doesn't happen often – certainly not on the Canal du Midi. Check first, though, that there are no stoppages in the region you plan to cruise. Much maintenance work takes place out of season.

Size of crew

Brochures may tell you that with a full complement of crew in the low season a boat can be hired for less than £45 per person per week. This could be true, but for the sake of remaining friends with the rest of your party, it is best to avoid the stress of overcrowding. Boating on quiet waterways with a 4 mph (6.5 kph) speed limit is one of the quickest ways to unwind and adjust to a gentler pace of life. Why spoil it by packing people in like battery hens? Follow the two-thirds rule – if there are four of you, get a boat for six or seven people.

Camping boats

Perhaps the exception to this general rule is the camping boat, usually a former working narrow boat with the hull covered in canvas. The holidaymakers in camping boats – teens and sub-teens, mostly – kip under the canvas and glory in crowding in together, Walkmans and all.

Boat design

Standards of hire craft are high today, but some are more thought-fully designed than others. Cast your eye over the seating layout. There may be, say, eight berths, but is there mealtime seating for eight? Or even for five or six? It can be tiresome to have to cook for two sittings. It is only at the planning stage of a holiday that the weather is consistently warm, sunny and dry, so you can't rely on dispatching half the crew to the roof or the towpath for a meal. Lounge and dining areas may have to be converted into sleeping cabins at night. Conversions for night-time use vary from simple to downright awkward. A seating fitment in a saloon may pull out in a couple of seconds to form a comfortable bunk without blocking off access to other parts of the boat. Lowering a table or fixing a board on which to arrange a jigsaw of mattresses to make a double bed can be time-consuming and obstructive and it is inconvenient to have the table out of commission.

Showers and flush toilets on board are no longer regarded as a luxury. They are accepted as standard. But is there room in the shower for you *and* a bath towel at the same time? And is there somewhere to keep the soap? Check the loo. It is sure to be perfectly clean, and the pump will work efficiently. But you'll have to be a contortionist if the toilet roll is fixed on the back wall.

What You Need

1 *Utensils* Crockery, cutlery and cooking utensils are provided on hire boats, but it's wise to check the inventory or you could set off for a week or two without a roasting tin or a casserole dish.

2 *Bedding* Duvets and/or sleeping bags will be found on board, but check with the operator if the brochure does not make it clear that sheets and towels are also provided. Some companies make a small extra charge for bed linen.

3 *Cutlery* Although most boatyards are meticulous about checking that everything is in its place, many share a curious blind spot about the quality of the contents of the cutlery drawer. In our experience it is quite rare to find an efficient tin opener, so maybe you should take your own. Boating in half a dozen countries in hired craft, we've yet to find a sharp bread knife or vegetable knife. Perhaps the boat operator is anxious to avoid bloodshed in the event of mutiny, but it is annoying to find the knife can't cope with the beautiful crusty loaf you've just bought.

Relaxing in the comfortable lounge/bar of *Le Sans Egal* at the end of a day cruising the royal River Thames

4 *Basic provisions* You will almost certainly need to take washing-up liquid and other cleaning products with you, as well as basics like pepper and salt and kitchen paper. Most hirers take over a boat on a Saturday afternoon and it could be Saturday night or Sunday before any deficiencies are discovered, which may mean it's Monday before you can shop. Many companies will have a box of groceries waiting on board if you request the service in advance. This is particularly helpful for holidaymakers arriving other than by car. If you're going to Amsterdam to pick up a boat in Friesland, say, you won't want to pack the ingredients of your weekend meals – in any case there are probably restrictions about importing meat and vegetable products.

5 *Nursery equipment* A young baby will be no trouble on board, and its range of equipment can be limited to essentials for a few days. A carrycot will be needed, but the galley sink can double as a baby bath, and the boat's movement is likely to soothe the infant. For those taking babies on a boating holiday, it's worth enquiring whether a hiring company can provide cot sides to fit to a bunk. Young babies are usually very contented on boats, but their accoutrements can take up more space than the rest of the crew's put together.

6 *Fishing tackle* Keen anglers will be furious if they forget their

fishing tackle – make sure the appropriate licences and permits are in order. You'll want to keep a photographic record of your holiday, but don't leave your camera on deck where it could be accidentally knocked overboard. You will need a fairly fast film to cope with some possibly rapid changes of light, from open country to well-wooded gorges and even concrete canyons. We've found that a camera can be used as an effective deterrent against hooligans. It's a regrettable fact that, mainly in some city areas, unruly youths seem to get pleasure from throwing missiles at passing boats, from the towpath or a bridge. They soon scarper when a camera is pointed at them – you don't even need to push the button.

7 *Television*   What about TV? We were appalled at the very idea for years, but succumbed when we hired out of season, in November, when cruising was impractical after 4 pm. The set was good company in the long evenings when we'd moored far from civilisation, and made a change from Scrabble. If you consider taking your own portable, rather than hiring from the yard, remember you'll need a set that operates from a 12 volt power system.

8 *Other useful items*   A torch is always useful on board. A floating one is ideal. A wooden, cork or plastic float will prevent your keys from sinking. See also below, *Safety First.*

What to Wear

Strong boots or shoes for walking on towpaths are better than wellingtons, which will fill with water and weigh you down if you fall in. Trainers make good deck shoes as long as the soles have not worn smooth. Slippery footwear is extremely dangerous on board a boat.

Jeans or shorts, a tee-shirt and sweater are the universal garb for boating. Young women may pack a bikini top, though this is considered superfluous by some, particularly in *la belle France.* Don't forget the suntan lotion! Take headgear to protect you from the sun and rain. Anyone sensitive to the glare from the water should take sunglasses. Wet weather gear is essential, especially for the stalwart outside at the helm.

Safety First

Things to do

- Pack insect-repellent and a basic first-aid kit to cope with bites, burns, blisters and cuts. These afflictions may give rise to the odd monosyllabic curse, but they are usually minor problems.
- If anyone falls in, put the engine into neutral instantly. Accidents are less likely to happen if you're aware of the risks. British Waterways, the authority responsible for most of Britain's waterways, publishes a free leaflet, the *Water Wise Code*, and while you're sending for it, also ask for the free booklet *Boating on the Waterways*, which outlines the important code of conduct. (See end of this chapter for the address.)
- Children and non-swimmers should, of course, wear lifejackets on board and on the towpath. Boat hire companies will supply them on request.
- Adapting to a confined space can take a little while, and for the first day or two on board the saloon echoes spasmodically to the thud of someone's head or shin contacting with solid steel, followed by a staccato oath. It shouldn't be necessary to resort to bikers' helmet or wicket-keeping pads. Most human beings eventually link effect with cause and avoid the confrontation. It is better to return home with a tan to flaunt to the neighbours, rather than the exotic blue, purple, yellow and magenta of massed bruises.

Things not to do

- Sprained ankles should be avoided at all costs. They are easily sustained, leaping ashore into long grass which conceals a hole in the towpath, or landing awkwardly on a mooring spike. They happen tediously often, and even without fractured bones can cause a crew member to be boat-bound and miserable for the duration.
- Take the greatest care not to fall in. There's nothing funny about slipping overboard, even when it happens to someone else. Churned-up canal or river water is an unsalubrious environment. Don't tell yourself: 'It's OK, he/she is a good swimmer.' It's no good being a strong swimmer if you're being swept like a feather over a lock sill or weir, or your foot is being sliced up by the propeller. To fall in at a lock – full or empty – has the added danger of being crushed between the boat and the lock wall.

• One tragedy in the Thames involved a strong swimmer who dived in to rescue his six-year-old son who had fallen overboard. The man struggled to remove his sweater in the water and was found drowned with the soaked garment over his head. The child doggy-paddled to the bank and safety.

What About Pets?

One big advantage of inland cruising – for Britons boating in Britain, anyway – is that pets can be taken along. Most boatyard operators allow at least one dog or cat, as long as it keeps to its own bed. The hamster or goldfish presents no problem. Cats can be surprisingly good cruising companions. Just let them investigate every nook and cranny, every drawer and locker, and they'll give their approval and settle down.

Dogs make great sailors, from the cocky little Yorkshire terrier to the Irish wolfhound who thinks he's the skipper. Once on board, poised on the bow or directing lock operations from the stern, the boating dog imagines himself a superior being, and expects no non-sense from any towpath tyke he encounters. He can make himself useful as ship's security officer.

As at home, don't let your dog run loose over farm land. He should, of course, have an identification tag on his collar, but for holiday use equip him also with one of those little screwtop tubes in which you can roll up a slip of paper bearing the name of the boat-hiring company and its phone number. Cats, too, should wear a collar with holiday address details.

Fuelling Up

Often the boat's fuel is included in the hire cost. Usually the fuel is marine diesel, and if you need to take on any from a waterside pump, you will be gratified to find that it costs less than half its price on a filling station forecourt.

Details of your hired craft may include the capacity of its water tank – up to 100 gals (3,785 l), maybe. If you think that's masses, you could be in for a surprise. Showers, washing-up sessions and cleaning the vegetables quickly lower the level in the tank, and you should top up the supply whenever a watering point is available. Likewise, get rid of rubbish whenever you can. It's amazing how quickly it accumulates. Whatever you do, *don't* throw it over the side or into a hedge. The commonest breakdowns on the waterways are caused by plastic bags fouling propellers.

Time to Cast Off

When you take over your craft, pay close attention to directions about gas appliances, engine maintenance, and keeping an eye on the weed hatch. It is most important that the skipper should be acquainted with the boat, and no self-respecting operator will let him leave the yard until he is. If you have any doubts *ask*.

Locks

Try to acquaint yourself with the working of locks before the big day. Read up on it, or watch other people doing it. Boatyard staff will explain it all to you, and ideally give a demonstration, but it's best to be prepared if possible. Locks are easy to work, though occasionally a paddle proves stiff to manipulate, and provide the opportunity to meet other addicts. But elderly boaters, or those not wanting too much physical exertion, may opt for the lockless Ashby Canal, near Coventry, or work out a route where locks are few and far between. The Norfolk Broads provide miles of lock-free cruising. On the River Thames and Continental waterways the locks are operated by keepers.

Ropes and knots

If you know nothing about knots, get a book or a cub scout to show you how to do a clove hitch and a round turn and two half hitches – the two most useful knots you'll need, and both easy to tie. Under way, keep lines neatly coiled on deck so that no one trips over them and they can be brought into instant use without having to be untangled. Fenders are meant to protect a boat's sides in a lock or on a mooring. It's good seamanship to bring them inboard when your vessel is on the move.

Refreshments

Sooner or later, you'll want to go ashore for a break and refreshment. Pubs which once turned their backs on the waterways have long since recognised the lucrative business which the cruising public has generated, and good bar snacks and meals are offered. Even at modest prices, these can be expensive for families, so the waterside grocery shops and cottages that sell dairy products and vegetables are welcome. At one time these were few and far between in the UK, but on most navigations today advance notices of a store round the next bend make self-catering easy.

Occasionally you come across a shop that stocks a whole range of canal paraphernalia – tea cloths, windlasses, sweaters, deck mops, bottled gas, Buckby cans – and these shops are bliss to browse in. There's usually an enormous book section, and it's wise to invest in one of the excellent charts in book form that detail every feature of a waterway that you're likely to encounter.

Right, are we ready to cast off?

Addresses

General information

British Waterways,
Melbury House,
Melbury Terrace,
London NW1 6JX
Tel: 01-725 8000

The Inland Waterways Association,
114 Regent's Park Road,
London NW1 8UQ

Brochures/reservations

Blakes Holidays Ltd,
Wroxham,
Norwich NR12 8DH
Tel: 06053 3221/2141

Boat Enquiries,
43 Botley Road,
Oxford
Tel: 0865 727288

Charter Cruising Company (hotel boats)
Unit 2, Rugby Wharf,
Consul Road,

Rugby,
Warwickshire CV21 1NR
Tel: 0788 69153

British Waterways Leisure,
Hire Cruiser Base,
Chester Road,
Nantwich,
Cheshire CW5 8LB
Tel: 0270 625122

Hoseasons Holidays,
Sunway House,
Lowestoft,
Suffolk NR32 3LT
Tel: 0502 500555

UK Waterway Holidays,
Welton Hythe,
Daventry,
Northants NN11 5LG
Tel: 0327 843773

Waterway Recovery Group,
Neil Edwards,
24A Avenue Road,
Witham,
Essex CM8 2DT
Tel: 0376 512977

WATERLUDE: THE LOCK KEEPER

Barry Whitelock, Bingley Five-Rise keeper

Barry Whitelock is keeper of the famous Bingley Five Rise staircase locks on the Leeds and Liverpool Canal and the Three Rise below them. A waterman from his distinctive peaked cap to the soles of his sturdy boots, he covers miles every day in summer, usually at a fast run. If he spots a schoolboy interfering with a paddle at the top lock he's up the flight in seconds. Each lock chamber in the Five Rise holds 80,000 gals (302,832 l) of water and can be emptied in three and a half minutes. As Barry explains, these locks need to be treated with caution . . .

'If you go wrong in these locks you can sink a boat in about thirty seconds,' says Barry. He doesn't suffer fools gladly, although he has a lot of time for people with a genuine interest in and respect for the canals generally and his section in particular. He also welcomes the parties of schoolchildren who visit him on waterway projects.

Most of the boaters encountering the impressive staircase locks which lift the Leeds and Liverpool Canal about 60 ft (18 m) at Bingley, near Bradford, are only too glad of Barry's help and advice. A few – usually experienced crews who claim to have worked more conventional locks than you've had hot dinners – think they've got the technique. But trouble can result from one false move. Barry, fit as a flea, runs up the steep flight dozens of times a day at peak season, and he has seen it all.

'My main duty is making sure the boating public use the locks properly. With two staircases in close proximity, people can easily go wrong if they don't listen to my instructions. I get a lot of boaters, especially from the Midlands, who think they've got a better idea than I have.'

No boater, no matter how experienced, is permitted to negotiate the Five Rise unsupervised, but Barry keeps a very close watch on the lower Three Rise locks, which need to be approached with great care. The problem is that the middle lock chamber is deeper than the one at the top. A boat going down can be grounded when water is transferred from the middle to the bottom lock. Unless care is exercised when more water is transferred from the top lock the boat can be sunk because it will be below the culverts.

'I've had to float boats off the bottom more than once,' says Barry. 'Trouble often arises because people are in too much of a hurry. I always tell boaters, before you do anything moor up, walk down and have a good look round the locks. Round here kids can leave a paddle open – and that's another thing that can put you on the bottom.

'One of the worst incidents I ever had was a 45-footer [13.5 m] and a 56-footer [17 m] on the bottom of the middle lock of the Three Rise on a Sunday morning. They were both hire boats coming uphill, and they failed to make sure the lock in front of them was full. It wasn't, and they emptied that half lock of water from the middle chamber down into the bottom lock, scraped over the sill, and got stuck on the bottom. The longer boat was actually stuck underneath the culvert of the nearside ground paddle.

'I put it down to inexperience and lack of instruction by the hire companies.

'Sunday afternoon can be murder, really, because the hire boats are eager to go, and this can be the first lock they come to. Some of them have been boating umpteen years down on the southern waters and they come here with a fixed system in their mind on how to do it. And I've got to stop them and try to explain that this is different. Some don't want to be told.

'What I normally do is leave a chamber down the staircase completely bone dry, and I tell them, "Right, if you don't set the staircase up properly, that's what you'll end up in!" They take it more seriously then.'

Barry deals with up to forty boats on what he terms a 'normal' day in the holiday season. 'My main traffic comes in spasms,' he says. 'I might get two hours without a boat, then I'll get five or six, all in one mad rush. On a Sunday, if the weather's good, I might have two or three hundred sightseers milling about the locks. This is a job that keeps you busy. You've got to have a lot of patience – and eyes in the back of your head.'

Born at nearby Shipley, Barry started work on a dairy farm – but his heart was always on the waterways. 'I've always been interested in boats, and I've been involved with the canal since I was about eight years old. When I left the farm I knew how to work these locks because on my half-day off I used to come and help the lock keeper, Eddie Murgatroyd. So when I first came on to the waterways I was a real relief lock keeper myself.

'I'm now a member of five boat clubs, including the Narrow Boat Owners' Club and the Bolinder Register, a kind of spares club for about a dozen of us who are Bolinder engine enthusiasts.'

The Bolinder, a diesel engine, is to canal traditionalists what the Spitfire is to World War II pilots. Barry's boat is a former Fellows Morton Company vessel which was recovered from the bottom of a canal, restored and shortened to 58 ft (17.4 m). It was built at Northwich in 1922 and is powered by a Bolinder.

Says Barry: 'I swear at mine to get her started, but once she's running she's all right for the day. I spend all my holidays on the boat. Married? No, I'm not married. I'm wed to my locks.'

NORTH WEST

Bingley's spectacular Five-Rise locks raise the Leeds and Liverpool Canal by 60 feet; one of the most magnificent feats of eighteenth-century engineering in Britain

Blackpool apart, possibly, the North West of England never enjoyed the best of reputations as a holiday area. To many people, this was the region of William Blake's 'dark, satanic mills'. At last, however, the situation is changing and holidaymakers are beginning to appreciate that the North West has much to offer: superb coastlines with beaches most people have to travel abroad to see, lakes, mountains, forests – and, of course, canals.

You could cruise around the region for weeks, crossing the Pennines from Lancashire into Yorkshire, or slipping from Cheshire to Staffordshire. And one thing you can be sure of is a variety of scenery – from the industrial areas of post-Industrial Revolution vintage to landscapes of sweet tranquillity and stunning beauty.

Leeds and Liverpool Canal

Completed in 1816, after forty-six years of stop-and-start construction, the Leeds and Liverpool Canal is the only trans-Pennine waterway link in operation today, although restoration work is in progress on both the Rochdale Canal and the Huddersfield Narrow Canal. It is hailed by many enthusiasts as one of the most scenic waterways in the United Kingdom and indeed it is for much of its length, but travelling from the western side boaters have a long, long way to go before they can appreciate it as such. In fact, it isn't until the summit level is reached at the top of Barrowford Locks that the canal takes on a truly rural character. That is a distance of some 80 miles (128 km), the first 35 miles (56 km) of which offer little in the way of boating holiday facilities. A popular starting point, therefore – and the one we have selected for this guide – is **Wigan**. That still involves a distance of 45 miles (72 km) and a rise of some 400 ft (120 m; 43 locks), or three days' solid cruising on a largely industrial section, but there is much of interest along the way.

A heavily industrialised town in a rather bleak mining area of Lancashire, Wigan has always been laughed at, and is the last place you might consider for the start of a holiday. Comedians poked fun at it in music halls before World War I – 20 miles (32 km) inland, and with its own pier! But Wigan Pier is no joke. Originally a coal staithe, it later served as a landing stage for passengers travelling between the town and Liverpool on horse-drawn packet boats. Today, it is one of the most successful tourist attractions in the country. In recent years an area of derelict warehouses surrounding the pier has been transformed into an absorbing museum exhibition entitled 'The

Wigan Pier

Way We Were'. This shows how people in the area lived and worked in the town's industrial heyday. For many visitors the museum highlight is the old schoolroom, locked in the time warp of a century ago, where they find themselves playing the role of pupils in the charge of a terrifying teacher in winged collar and frock-tailed coat, bending a wicked-looking cane as he makes them chant multiplication tables and sing hymns. It is all enormous fun. Also on the site is a large pub, The Orwell, honouring George Orwell and his book *The Road to Wigan Pier*, and an interesting gift shop.

Wigan Metropolitan Council operates electric water buses between the pier and Trencherfield Mill, where there are moorings a quarter of a mile (0.4 km) from the town centre. A British Waterways' short boat alongside the mill houses another small exhibition. The short boats were wide-beam but restricted to 62 ft (18.6 m) in length to negotiate locks on the Leeds and Liverpool east of Wigan. They operated as a pair – motor towing the butty – like the narrow boats further south. Opposite the mill is a boatyard offering all the usual facilities.

The first two locks encountered on the journey east – just beyond Wigan Pier – will take full-length narrow boats of 72 ft (21.6 m). Just after the second lock, peeling off to the south and overshadowed by Wigan power station, is the canal's Leigh Branch which connects with the Bridgewater Canal 7 miles (11 km) away. And just ahead, around a corner, is the first of the infamous Wigan 21.

The average crew will take about five hours to get a boat up the Wigan 21. Overnight mooring is not allowed in the short pounds – skippers who ignore this restriction could well find their boats on the mud the following morning, due to leaky lock gates or vandalism – so it is inadvisable to start late in the afternoon. Many of the locks are especially deep, so make sure ropes are long enough to reach the bollards. Ground paddles on the locks need to be approached with great caution. Raise the ground paddles first and wait until the boat has risen a few feet before winding up the gate paddles. It is possible for a boat to be sunk in the violent gush of water which surges from the gates. The upper half of the flight is very open to the wind, so again care is needed. Take heart, though – at the top there are good moorings and three pubs within easy walking distance.

The next 10-mile (16 km) stretch was once shared with the Lancaster Canal Company. It passes through the grounds of **Haigh Hall**, a reconstructed pre-Tudor mansion. The grounds include a nature trail and a golf course and are open to the public. The canal winds on through the busy towns of Adlington and Chorley before reaching **Johnson's Hill Locks**, a pretty flight of seven. There is a watering point at the top, and a watering hole for the thirsty crew.

Withnell Fold is an interesting village that could easily be overlooked, but it is worth a brief stop. At one time it could have been described as a capitalist's capital, for its paper mills, now defunct, supplied the raw material upon which many of the world's bank notes were printed. At the centre of the village a set of stocks stands as a warning to counterfeiters, if no one else.

On then to **Blackburn**, and it is a shame that although this canal is generally deeper than most of the narrow waterways it contains an awful lot of rubbish. Your boat is unlikely to 'touch bottom', or even run aground, but the propeller may become entangled with rubber tyres, supermarket trolleys, barbed wire, rope, articles of clothing, mattresses, dead dogs and more plastic than you could possibly imagine. Blackburn has six locks, kept in good order, and from the second lock it is a fifteen-minute walk to the town centre, a reasonable place to shop. It takes a long time to cruise through the town and an overnight stay is not recommended, so skippers need to think about their timings.

Beyond Blackburn the canal twists and turns around the hillsides of the Calder Valley, sharing its course with a motorway that is sometimes difficult to ignore. The 559 yds (503 m) long Gannow Tunnel leads boats into the centre of **Burnley**, where the waterway, passing through an impressively preserved area known as the Weavers' Triangle, is quite enchanting, despite the rubbish. The toll house beside the canal is an information centre and museum. Boaters can moor near here and take a walk around the mills. Just beyond the British Waterways maintenance yard is the start of the 60 ft (18 m) high Burnley Embankment which carries the canal over the town for a distance of three-quarters of a mile. There are moorings here, but the safest place is not on the ever-active towpath side. There is a more private position near the Calder aqueduct with bollards to tie up to, still only a quarter of a mile from the town centre.

Burnley gradually becomes Brierfield which in turn merges with Nelson, last of the Lancashire towns actually on the waterway. At last the seven Barrowford Locks are reached and ahead lies countryside of the sort only the Leeds and Liverpool can offer: a landscape of stone-built moorland farms and the distant mountains of the Pennine Chain. **Foulridge** (pronounced 'fullridge') Tunnel, 1,640 yds (1,476 m) long, has a one-way system controlled by traffic lights because wide-beam boats still use the canal. At times it may take an hour for the lights to change. However, patience may be rewarded at the other end in the bar of the Hole in the Wall pub, where there are photographs of an incident in 1912 when a cow fell in at one end of the tunnel and swam through to the other, where it was pulled out and given a stiff drink. Another pub with an unusual feature is the Anchor Inn at **Salterforth**. If he's not too busy, ask the landlord to show you the stalactites. They're in the cellar.

The inevitable descent starts about a mile after cruising through the outskirts of Barnoldswick with the three locks at Greenberfield. The flight was re-routed in the 1820s, but the original course can still be seen. Soon after passing through Bridge 159, downstream of the Greenberfield bottom lock, the waterway crosses the border into North Yorkshire. There are many tight bends along this pound and many have bridges on them, calling for careful navigation. Murphy's Law dictates that an oncoming boat will almost certainly be met in a bridgehole on a bend.

At **East Marton** you will probably begin to notice booted and backpacked hikers striding along the towpath. For a short distance the towpath is part of the the rugged Pennine Way, a challenging 250-mile (400 km) walking route along the spine of England. The village is a pleasurable stop with moorings either side of a curious double bridge, the result of road improvements which set one arch atop another. There is a pub, the Cross Keys, selling real ales, bar snacks and full meals, and a farmhouse shop offering good local produce to passing boaters. After East Marton the canal follows a contour line in a huge 'W' shape. This provides the odd experience of seeing a boat apparently approaching you a field or so away that is probably twenty minutes or so *ahead* of you.

Bank Newton, in a superb, wooded setting, brings a flight of six locks that lower the canal 56 ft (17 m) to set it on a rather straighter course across upper Airedale. For crew members fancying a change of activity, there are riding stables at Bank Newton. Moor near the bridge before the locks, cross over and follow the lane for a short distance. Don't worry if you have never ridden before – there are experienced, sympathetic instructors.

Soon after the Bank Newton Six the canal crosses the River Aire on the Priest Holme aqueduct, and a further six single locks – the first since the other side of Wigan – drop through **Gargrave** and on to a 17-mile (27 km) lock-free stretch. There's no chance of anyone's muscles going flabby, though – there are a good many swing bridges on this pound, some quite heavy. Gargrave, a picturesque village with attractive stone cottages and three pubs, is a worthwhile stop. The waterway skirts the Yorkshire Dales National Park as it winds on towards **Skipton**.

An attractive town, Skipton draws many tourists in the summer, but for boaters, at least, there is plenty of room. There are many

Hire boats get a change-over clean-up at Skipton

moorings within a two-minute walk of the town centre, including some along the 770 yds (693 m) long Springs Branch, which leads off towards the castle. The branch was built at the end of the eighteenth century to transport limestone from a nearby quarry. It's a pleasant place in which to moor, but turning space is tight for boats longer than 35 ft (10.5 m). There is a launderette not far from the moorings. Just outside Skipton at Snaygill Bridge there is a canalside pub with a large family room and a spacious garden. On the opposite side is the tidy, well-kept boatyard belonging to Snaygill Boats. The canal continues on a pleasant course along the Aire valley through Kildwick and Silsden. It would be a good idea to have someone permanently ahead on the towpath, operating the swing bridges which are now very frequent.

At **Stockbridge** you can moor opposite the Marquis of Granby for a visit to East Riddlesden Hall, a traditional seventeenth-century West Yorkshire manor house with panelled rooms, fine plasterwork and mullioned windows. Ancient domestic utensils, pewter ware and Yorkshire oak furniture are displayed. There is a medieval barn with a collection of traditional agricultural machinery and a 'stew pond' in which monks of old kept their fish fresh for the pot. Another option is to take the steam train from Keighley station into the Brontë Country. From Haworth station board an open top bus for a circular tour around the moors. Both services run regularly throughout the day during the summer. Haworth Parsonage, former home of the strangely gifted sisters, is now a museum and well worth a visit.

And so to **Bingley**. The Bingley Five Rise Locks, a staircase which lifts boats 60 ft (18 m) are always a hive of activity, with thousands of visitors every year. Working the locks is quite an experience, but wait for the lock keeper's assistance. The Three Rise staircase a little further on has confused many experienced boaters because the chambers are not of equal size. Below the Three Rise are moorings handy for the town centre. The canal continues through pleasantly wooded surroundings to Saltaire, an appealing village built in the 1850s by Sir Titus Salt, a prosperous mill owner who felt his employees deserved more than the bleak terraces in which such workers were customarily housed. Mellow stone mill buildings alongside the canal house an art gallery and museum initiated by the artist David Hockney.

The open countryside which has been such a feature of the Leeds and Liverpool for so long begins to dwindle. Nevertheless, although the scenery becomes more built-up, there are wooded areas and the canal retains its independence almost into the heart of Leeds where it joins the Aire and Calder Navigations, with links to the waterways of the North East and South Yorkshire.

Shropshire Union Canal

Passing through rocky, leafy cuttings, high bridges of fine masonry and between lush green meadows, the Shropshire Union follows a more or less straight course from Ellesmere Port on the estuary of the River Mersey to Wolverhampton in the heart of the English Midlands. In this chapter we shall be tracing it only as far as Barbridge, Cheshire, where the Middlewich Branch strikes off to join the Trent and Mersey 10 miles (16 km) away. We will deal with this branch and the remainder of the 'Shroppie', as aficionados affectionately term it, in our chapter on the Four Counties Ring.

Originally, the Shroppie was four canals: the Wirral Line of the Ellesmere Canal which opened in 1795 from Ellesmere Port to Chester, where it connected with the Chester Canal which had been running from Chester to Nantwich since 1779; the Middlewich Branch which the Chester and Ellesmere Canal Company opened between Barbridge and Middlewich in 1833, and the Birmingham and Liverpool Junction Canal which opened from Nantwich to Autherley Junction, on the northern outskirts of Wolverhampton, in 1835.

Situated among the chemical plants and oil refineries of the Mersey Estuary, **Ellesmere Port** ought not to be of much interest to any leisure boater, yet hundreds follow the drab route from Chester each year on what can only be described as a pilgrimage. Their shrine is the Boat Museum at Ellesmere Port, a unique collection of inland waterways vessels afloat in the basin, surrounded by buildings housing an indoor exhibition of canal history, artefacts and engineering gadgetry. Opened in 1976, with the Tom Rolt Education and Conference Centre, honouring the author of *Narrow Boat* and a founder of the Inland Waterways Association, being added in 1984, the Boat Museum is constantly expanding.

Chester, the only English city with its ancient walls more or less intact, is a massive tourist attraction, and in high summer its quaint streets, The Rows, with medieval two-storey shopping, are packed with visitors. Take a walk right round the walls and you will cover two miles. There is no shortage of moorings. The River Dee is not far from the canal and a number of passenger boats operate on both waterways. Access by boat to the Dee is not easy. The Section

Inspector at Tower Wharf, Chester, has to be given at least 48 hours' notice of intention to enter the Dee Branch, which has three locks. The last one, giving direct access to the Dee, can only be negotiated an hour either side of high water. On the canal, below Northgate Locks, the Chester Packet Boat Company offers trips in a horse-drawn boat, a sight rarely seen these days as horses are not usually allowed on the towpaths which were originally intended for their use.

Five locks rise out of Chester to Christleton and on to an eight-mile lock-free section. Just beyond the first bridge after Christleton Lock is Ye Old Trooper, a large pub/restaurant with handy moorings. The canal now takes a winding course through Cheshire farmland. The rather flat countryside is mitigated by distant hills ahead, crowned by **Beeston Castle** perched craggily 300 ft (90 m) above the Cheshire Plain. Glared at from the south by the turrets of Peckforton Castle, Beeston is open to the public. It's a half-mile (0.8 m) walk from Bridge 109, beside which is the Shady Oak pub, where you might well be glad of a little refreshment after the trip ashore.

The village of **Beeston** has two locks, one with an iron chamber. Its original walls were not strong enough so iron was used to prevent subsidence. Below the lock is a small boatyard owned by Chas Hardern & Co. which runs a small fleet of narrow boats for hire. It also has a small but well-stocked canal shop, one of the best in the region. The yard is a pleasant alternative mooring for those wishing to visit Beeston Castle, though the climb from here is rather more strenuous. At the stone lock is a shop selling good home produce. After wooded Tilstone Lock comes the two-rise Bunbury staircase beyond which a busy boatyard operated by Dartline offers small electric narrow boats for hire by the day – a good way to 'test the water' before committing oneself to a week or more afloat. Dartline's workshops here were stables in the days of horse-drawn boats when Bunbury was an important canal centre.

A popular overnight mooring place is **Barbridge**, where the Middlewich Branch of the Shroppie heads off towards Middlewich. Just beyond the junction, on the opposite side of the canal, is the Barbridge Inn which serves real ale and real food in a bustling indoor and outdoor setting. Good moorings on either side, but try to arrive early for the best ones, of course.

Lancaster Canal

Set apart from the rest of the system, the Lancaster Canal traverses a winding and at times extremely attractive route sandwiched between the mountains of the Pennine Chain and the waters of the Irish Sea. It starts not far from the Ribble Estuary and ends within sight of the Lake District's foothills. It crosses The Fylde, Lancashire's great 'salad bowl' area of glasshouses and market gardens, and comes within a wave's whisper of the sea in Morecambe Bay.

The Lancaster covers just over 41 miles (67 km) between the outskirts of Preston and its terminus just above the village of Borwick. There are no locks on the main line – swing bridges tone up the muscles instead – but the 2¾-mile (4.4 km) Glasson Branch which heads for the Lune Estuary 24 miles (38 km) from Preston has six, each one taking boats up to 72 ft (22 m) long by 14 ft (4.2 m) wide.

Completed in 1799, the canal was built to provide a link between the fertile agricultural region of northern Lancashire and the increasingly populous industrial areas of Merseyside and Manchester, shipping coal in one direction and farm produce in the other. By 1819 it had been extended some 12 miles (19 km) from Tewitfield, its present terminus, to the Lake District town of Kendal. Soon, special 'fly' boats were providing an express passenger service, covering the distance between Preston and Kendal in a mere eight hours. During the 1930s the northern end of the canal was shortened and each of the eight locks that climbed up to Kendal fell into disuse. In 1968 the Tewitfield locks were closed for good to make way for the M6 motorway.

None of the boatyards operating hire craft on the Lancaster is very keen on boats being taken into Preston, where the canal makes a sullen start in Ashton Basin and slinks through the suburbs before making a dash for the open country beyond the village of Salwick. Holidaymakers are more likely to start from Catforth, 7 miles (11 km) north of Preston, where there are two hire boat companies. **Garstang**, a further 9 miles (14 km) to the north, makes an attractive overnight stop. It is a small market town with a cobbled market square. There are moorings in Garstang Basin where restored wharf buildings house a restaurant and a museum. The canal is overlooked by the ruins of Greenhalgh Castle, built in 1490, reduced to rubble by Roundheads during the Civil War. There is good walking country in the Pennine slopes west of the town.

The **Glasson** Branch leads off to the left just before the village of Galgate where a mill has been spinning silk since 1792, the year construction work was started on the canal. The branch was completed in 1826 to provide a direct link between the Lancaster and the sea. Until then, cargoes had been trans-shipped between barges and coastal vessels at Hest Bank, 5 miles (8 km) north of Lancaster, where the canal passes within 200 yds (180 m) of the coast. The six locks drop the canal a total of 52 ft (15.6 m) to the busy little port of Glasson, still making a living from commercial shipping, though the basin is now full of pleasure craft. Entrance between the basin and the tidal River Lune can be made only at high water. Glasson Dock is an interesting and attractive spot and there is a good mariners' pub. From the dock you can walk along the windswept coast to the ruined Cockersand Abbey.

Back at Galgate, the main line continues north to Lancaster, crossing lovely, rolling countryside and passing through a long wooded cutting to reach the outskirts of the old county town. Dominated by Lancaster Castle, with the tower known as John of Gaunt's Chair, the town has waterside architecture – on both canal and River Lune – which provides much evidence of the days when it was a major port. Crews stopping here will find plenty to keep them occupied. There is an intriguing maze of old alleyways and a Shire Hall with a collection of six hundred heraldic shields. Lancaster Museum, in Market Square, houses prehistoric, Roman and medieval exhibits as well as collections of pottery, porcelain, firearms and paintings.

The canal leaves Lancaster by way of two aqueducts – the first crosses the A683 road and the next, a sturdy but dignified original from the time when the waterway was built, strides grandly across the Lune. Now the canal edges ever closer to Morecambe Bay, and at Hest Bank it is easy to see why this was the place chosen for the trans-shipment of cargoes in the days before the Glasson Branch was cut. At **Bolton-le-Sands** the Packet Boat Hotel is a reminder of the time when the 'fly' boats used to stop here. Today, Bolton-le-Sands is an attractive dormitory village and quiet resort.

The last place of any size on the Lancaster Canal is **Carnforth**, not the town with the biggest tourism pull in the world, but it is an important rail junction and it is the home of Steamtown, a railway museum with classic locos – including the legendary Flying Scotsman – set up on 5 miles (8 km) of track. From Carnforth the canal meanders 4 miles (6 km) to Borwick where it is overlooked, rather glumly, by an Elizabethan manor. The navigation ends quite suddenly just before it reaches the old Tewitfield Locks.

Addresses

North West Tourist Board,
The Last Drop Village,
Bromley Cross,
Bolton BL7 9PZ
Tel: 0204 591511

Yorkshire and Humberside Tourist Board,
312 Tadcaster Road,
York YO2 2HF
Tel: 0904 707961

Leeds and Liverpool Canal

Brochures/reservations

Black Prince Holidays Ltd (base at Silsden)
Stoke Prior,
Bromsgrove,
Worcestershire B60 4LA
Tel: 0527 575115

IML Waterway Cruising Ltd
Bank Newton,
Near Skipton,
North Yorks BD23 3NT
Tel: 0756 749492

L & L Cruisers,
Rawlinson Lane,
Heath Charnock,
Chorley,
Lancs PR7 4DE
Tel: 0257 480825

Pennine Cruisers,
19 Coach Street,
Skipton,
North Yorks BD23 1LH

Rodley Boat Centre,
Canal Wharf,
Canal Road,
Rodley,
Leeds LS13 1LN
Tel: 0532 576132

Snaygill Boats Ltd,
Skipton Road,
Bradley,
Skipton,
Yorks BD20 9HA
Tel: 0756 5150

Wayfarer Narrow Boats Ltd,
Swan Meadow Road,
Wigan,
Lancs WN3 5BG
Tel: 0942 41890

Shropshire Union Canal

Brochures/reservations

Dartline Cruisers,
10 Canal Wharf,
Bunbury,
Tarporley,
Cheshire CW6 9QB
Tel: 0829 260638

Chas Hardern and Co.,
Beeston Castle Wharf,
Beeston,
Near Tarporley,
Cheshire CW6 9NH
Tel: 0829 32595

Holiday-Makers (Cheshire) Ltd,
Waverton Mill,
Eggbridge Lane,
Waverton,
Chester CH3 7PE
Tel: 0244 336456/7

Lancaster Canal

Brochures/reservations

Adventure Cruisers,
The Jolly Roger,
Catforth,
Preston,
Lancs PR4 0HE
Tel: 0772 690232

Canal Cruises,
Penny Street,
Bridge Wharf,
Lancaster LA1 1XN
Tel: 0253 293966

Nu-Way Acorn,
Preston Street,
Carnforth,
Lancs LA5 9BY
Tel: 0524 734457

Preston Hire Cruisers,
Moons Bridge Wharf,
Hollowforth Lane,
Woodplumpton,
Preston,
Lancs
Tel: 0772 690627

CHESHIRE RING

Barton Aqueduct, Bridgewater Canal

Whatever anyone may tell you, allow two weeks to complete the very popular Cheshire Ring. An experienced crew, going flat out to make the most of daylight during high summer, can do it in a week – and then, probably, only if they are taking part in a sponsored contest of some sort. Many a boating holiday has been ruined because skipper and crew have tried to cover too much ground in too little time.

The Cheshire Ring covers six canals – the Bridgewater, Trent and Mersey, Macclesfield, Peak Forest, Ashton and Rochdale – and during the circuit you will clock up just over 100 miles (160 km). Since it is a circular route, you can go in either direction, of course, and there are a number of starting points along the way. But for the sake of starting somewhere, we have chosen the Manchester area as a convenient place to reach and an anti-clockwise direction to avoid some strenuous lock work at the start of a trip.

Bridgewater Canal

The Bridgewater Canal, named after the entrepreneur who master-minded its concept, Francis Egerton, 3rd Duke of Bridgewater, expresses the dynamism of Britain's Industrial Revolution. It was originally intended to ship coal to Manchester from the Duke's mines a few miles away at Worsley, but things happened fast in the second half of the eighteenth century and the canal finally became one of the most important waterways in the country, not only linking Liverpool and Manchester, but also connecting with the trans-Pennine Leeds and Liverpool Canal to the north and the Trent and Mersey Canal to the south.

The most notable feature of the Bridgewater Canal is that throughout its length – 23½ miles (38 km) on the main line and just over 14 miles (23 km) on the Leigh and Runcorn Branches – there are no locks. The engineers who designed it, James Brindley and John Gilbert, chose a contour course, using aqueducts to cross valleys and depressions, and they also made it the first canal in Britain to run independently of natural watercourses.

The Bridgewater is a very satisfactory waterway to navigate. It passes through landscapes ranging from the commercial heart of Manchester to scenes of pastoral beauty. It is undiminished by the steaming industrial sprawl of Trafford Park, and it enhances the suburban and semi-rural character of places like Lymm and Grappenhall. It even adds a touch of eighteenth-century grace to the uncompromisingly twentieth-century nuclear science research

The Grocers' Warehouse in the Bridgewater Canal Basin. The building was demolished in the 1960s and has recently been partially rebuilt by Manchester City Council

laboratory at Daresbury, a couple of miles from Preston Brook, the canal's southern terminus.

Leigh Branch

The Bridgewater Canal officially starts (or finishes, if you prefer) at Castlefield Junction in the centre of Manchester, but since there are no hire boat facilities in this area and it is an unlikely starting place for a voyage, we'll take a look first at the Leigh Branch, which connects with the Leeds and Liverpool Canal.

The branch starts at **Leigh**, 7 miles (11 km) from Wigan, dominated by factory chimneys, and set in cotton mill and colliery country. This is exactly the sort of place canals were designed to serve; a place that needed fuel bringing in and products taking out. Between Leigh and Worsley the countryside has that gaunt, pinched look of many spent northern industrial areas – a near wasteland of rusting winding gear and derelict buildings with pieces of corrugated iron flapping and clattering in the breeze. But it is peaceful for all that, and it is safe to leave the boat moored up while you go ashore at Astley Green, for instance, where there are a few shops and a couple of pubs.

Worsley, the original raison d'être for the Bridgewater, is a surprising place. The M62, as restless as any motorway, crosses the canal here, and at weekends especially the air is filled with the relentless buzzing of light aircraft from the nearby Barton Aerodrome, but Worsley is a delightful village with a large green, ancient black-and-white timbered houses and pleasant moorings handy for shops and the large and busy Bridgewater Hotel. The canal water here is a bright ochre colour, the result of iron ore in the local rock.

Worsley is distinguished as the birthplace of British canals. The Bridgewater was not the first waterway, of course, but it was the first true canal, and it happened because of coal, which had been mined in the village since the fourteenth century. An extraordinary aspect to the building of the Bridgewater is that simultaneously the Duke of Bridgewater developed an underground canal system – on two levels – to bring the coal straight from the face. An ingenious inclined plane lifted boats up and down a one-in-four gradient at one point in the mine, and the underground waterway system eventually totalled 46 miles (74 km). Worsley Delph, the old canal basin, is still there, serving as a winding hole, just opposite an attractive old timbered house, where the canal does a dog's leg turn after passing under the M62 and the village bridge. It is possible to navigate the mine's entrance tunnels.

There are two hire boatyards at Worsley – one in Blake's consortium, the other Hoseasons – and the village is a good starting point for both the Cheshire Ring and the Leeds and Liverpool Canal.

South of Worsley, the canal drifts through urban Patricroft to Barton-upon-Irwell, gradually losing its reddish tinge. For a time, road and waterway are on a level, side by side, then you round a bend, pass a pub, an old cotton mill and a boatyard, and the road falls away. You are about to be confronted by one of the engineering wonders of the 1790s – the 234 ft (70 m) long **Barton Swing Aqueduct** which carries the Bridgewater over the Manchester Ship Canal. Crossing the aqueduct is a dramatic experience: its vermilion girders, reflected in the water, stand like the gateway of an ancient city, and it is an eerie, insecure sensation to be floating – flying, it seems – above the ship canal some 50 ft (15 m) below. The aqueduct weighs 800 tons (806,400 kg) and swings at right angles, pivoting on a central island to allow the passage of shipping along the ship canal. Gates seal off each end of the aqueduct and the Bridgewater.

Beyond the aqueduct the Bridgewater trudges a dreary couple of miles through the vast loading bays and factories of Trafford Park – lots and lots of anglers along this stretch during the coarse fishing season – but it manages to retain its identity, even though chain link fences keep it apart from the kind of industrial environment it was intended to serve.

The Leigh Branch joins the main line at a place with the apt but whimsical name of Waters Meeting. It has a Tolkien ring about it: a place guarded by elves, perhaps, with harp music drifting from banks of sweet-scented wild flowers.

Turn left for Manchester city centre, right for Sale and Altrincham. And mind that supermarket trolley dumped in the cut . . .

Bridgewater Canal (Main Line)

Boaters travel through **Manchester** for one reason only: to complete the Cheshire Ring by way of the Rochdale Canal, which in turn gives access to the Ashton, Peak Forest and Macclesfield Canals. But Manchester is worth an overnight stop, if only to justify the punishing fee which has to be paid to the Rochdale Canal Company for using two miles of its water. This fee is *not* usually included in boat rental contracts, so if you are doing the Ring be prepared to fork out. Hooligans apart – there are safe moorings near Castlefield – the city does have its attractive side. There are lots of pubs and restaurants, and there is Castlefield itself, claimed by the North West Tourist Board as 'Britain's First Urban Heritage Park'. Site of the Roman fort from which Mancunium gained its name, Castlefield was the heart of the canal and railway systems during the city's industrial heyday. The area fell into decline this century, but a progressive local authority has revived it with imaginative landscaping and by opening up museums and exhibitions and a visitors' centre. Within easy walking distance are the Granada TV Studios where visitors can tour Coronation Street and other well-known sets.

The Rochdale Canal starts with a lock just to the east of Castlefield, and a short distance to the east is Hulme Lock, which provides access to the Manchester Ship Canal and the River Irwell. Special conditions have to be met before pleasure craft are allowed to use the ship canal. Between Castlefield and Waters Meeting there is little to remark on, except perhaps for the benefit of football and cricket fans, who might like to know that the Bridgewater Canal passes close to both Manchester United's ground and Old Trafford. Otherwise, unless you are deeply into industrial architecture of the post-prefabricated factory era there's little to do but head for that supermarket trolley at Waters Meeting.

Stretford, Ashton Upon Mersey, Sale and Altrincham have to be endured as the canal heads almost due south for the next 6 miles (10 km) or so, but there are a few landmarks along the way, including two canalside pubs – the Bridge Inn at Dane Road bridge, and The Railway at Sale bridge. Sighting the Linotype factory, another monument to Victorian technology, just below Broadheath bridge, tells you that the canal is about to take a westerly course, away from the sprawling suburbs of Greater Manchester, towards the fresher air and greener grass of Cheshire.

As the countryside becomes more rural, you can appreciate the surveying skills that went into choosing the Bridgewater's route. To the west of Dunham Town, below the canal, is **Dunham Massey Hall**, a National Trust property with deer roaming its wooded parkland. The hall was formerly the seat of the Earl of Stamford, and boaters can moor up in Bollington to visit it if they wish. On sunny summer weekends they might prefer to sail nonchalantly above the bumper-to-bumper traffic heading for the car park. A modern aqueduct, built to replace the original stone construction which was badly damaged in 1971, carries boats over the River Bollin, and as the canal enters a sharp turn to the right there is an opportunity for liquid replenishment for both boat and crew. On the left bank is a watering point, and on the road just below it an attractive pub with the intriguing name of Ye Olde No 3. And remember, please don't leave your boat moored in front of the tap if you go to the pub.

Lymm, halfway mark along the Bridgewater's main line, is a great canal centre. Small town, large village – call it what you will – it's a place where all roads, it seems, lead to, over or under The Cut. There is a very lively local boat club, as the number of occupied moorings on the approaches to Lymm will testify, and the passage through the town is most attractive. Several houses have frontages on to the towpath, and the canal travels over and through ravines of sandstone. There is a wide choice of pubs and restaurants in Lymm, as well as one or two supermarkets and some good, old-fashioned corner shops.

You might decide to moor overnight in Lymm, but if you prefer somewhere rather quieter – not that Lymm is any Tower of Babel – then Grappenhall, a further hour's cruising, would be worth considering. This is the English village at its best: the canal overhung by shady trees, a genteel, eighteenth-century stone bridge and a cobble-stoned street with two excellent pubs, the Ram's Head and the Parr

Arms. The parish church has splendid stained-glass windows, best seen from outside at night with the church's interior lights lit.

West of Grappenhall Bridge, the canal emerges from its screen of trees to travel between open fields on one side and red-brick suburbia on the other. **Stockton Heath** looks unpromising from its outskirts and the map, but the town centre has a surprisingly attractive waterfront on each bank. Combining new properties with existing waterfront buildings, the planners have managed to retain something of the atmosphere of the place when it was the terminus before the Bridgewater was completed to Runcorn. It is a busy area, lively with leisure use, and you would scarcely believe that Stockton Heath is on the edge of industrial Warrington.

The canal soon becomes rural again, passing the villages of Higher Walton and Moore, both with pleasant moorings, good pubs and handy shops, before reaching the neatly manicured lawns and clinical architecture of the nuclear science research laboratory at **Daresbury**. The village, attractively set on a hillside, is about half a mile (0.8 km) from the canal, behind the laboratory. It is the birthplace of Lewis Carroll, who is featured with some of the characters from *Alice in Wonderland* in a memorial window in the local church.

The sight of the M56 bridge striding across the canal tells us that the main line is coming to an end. Just before the bridge, on the right, is the Runcorn Arm of the Bridgewater, snaking its way eastwards towards its original destination. At Runcorn there used to be locks connecting the canal with the River Mersey, but these were closed in 1966.

Preston Brook, just the other side of the motorway bridge, belongs very much to the canal era. This was where cargoes from the wide-beamed vessels of Manchester and the North West and those carried by narrow boats from the Midlands were trans-shipped. Two marinas, one of them a hire boat centre, help to retain something of its atmosphere as a port.

Few boaters can approach Preston Brook without experiencing a mounting sense of excitement as the canal flows towards its terminus at the mouth of the Preston Brook Tunnel, 1,239 yds (1,115 m) long, and the start of another historic and exciting waterway.

Trent and Mersey Canal

The Trent and Mersey was originally known, more poetically, as the Grand Trunk Canal. For more than 140 years – from its opening in

1777 to the end of the First World War – it flourished as a commercial artery, connecting with nine other major waterways along its 93-mile (149 km) route to Derwent Mouth, near Long Eaton in Nottinghamshire. In this section, however, we will be looking only at the first 29 miles (46 km), as far as Kidsgrove, Staffordshire, where the Trent and Mersey connects with the Macclesfield Canal for the next stage of the Cheshire Ring.

The canal was a success right from the start, transporting china clay from the port of Liverpool straight to the factories of the Potteries. Among its main sponsors, not surprisingly, was Josiah Wedgwood, one of a group of industrial visionaries whose insight brought new trade and prosperity to the English North West and Midlands. Popular with leisure boaters, the Trent and Mersey remains an important waterway to this day. Although there are some industrial eyesores along the way, its route is largely serene and beautiful. At its northern end, however, it begins in darkness.

Preston Brook Tunnel is not wide enough for two boats to pass each other, so during the main boating season a timetable posted at each end controls alternating one-way traffic. At other times of the year it's best to approach the tunnel with caution. You can just see through to the other end, and you should, in any event, be able to see the headlight of an approaching boat. You will also most probably hear shouts of something like 'Left, right – right a bit more,' as a lookout in the bows of a narrow boat directs the person on the tiller. Steering a straight course can be quite difficult in a tunnel.

After some twenty minutes of echoing gloom, the boat emerges into a scene of sylvan tranquillity, and it wouldn't be too fanciful to imagine oneself in a totally different country. Just ahead lies Dutton stop lock where boaters in the past paid their dues to the canal authority. It takes little time to negotiate the lock: it was erected to halt boats rather than lift them to a different level. The first real lock is some 16 miles (26 km) ahead. But there are two more tunnels to negotiate as the Trent and Mersey snakes along the hillsides of the Weaver Valley. Boaters will see spectacular views of the River Weaver Navigation, far below on the right.

The two tunnels are relatively short – Saltersford is 424 yds (382 m) long, and Barnton, very soon afterwards, 572 yds (515 m) – but they can be tricky. Each has a kink and is wide enough for only one boat. And as you leave Saltersford Tunnel at the Barnton end take care to keep to the right-hand side of the channel. A nasty sand bar reaches out from the left.

Soon after the village of Barnton you come to a marvel of canal engineering – the **Anderton Boat Lift**. Built in 1875, the lift carried

Industrial reflections, Northwich, Trent and Mersey Canal

boats up and down the 50 ft (15 m) incline between the Trent and Mersey and the River Weaver. The boats were transported in counterbalanced water-filled tanks, and the whole hydraulic operation was designed by Edwin Clark, who five years later was asked to design a similar lift at Les Fontinettes on the Canal de Neuffossé, a rare French tribute to British skill. Sadly, the Anderton lift is no longer in use, although an active lobby of waterways enthusiasts is striving to save it.

The countryside between Anderton and Lostock Gralam, on the outskirts of **Northwich**, continues to be rural, but the ground's 'lumpy' appearance is the result of industry underground, for this is a salt mining area. Chemical plants dominate the scenery at Northwich with pipe bridges and gaunt ironwork structures crossing the canal and plumes of steam stark against the sky. There is a strange beauty about it all, however, and there are opportunities for taking some very striking photographs. At Lostock Gralam look for the electric narrow boat operated as a trip boat by the Colliery Narrow Boat Company – a very elegant craft.

Broken Cross, a suburb of Northwich, marks the start of another rural stretch. Surrounded by a neatly grassed area, the Old Broken Cross pub beckons invitingly, the last chance of canalside refreshment until Middlewich, 5 miles (8 km) away. Salt mine subsidence has left its mark on the canal south of Broken Cross in the form of a number of lagoons, sad with the semi-submerged hulks of old narrow boats, but rich in birdlife. There are herons galore, of course, but sharp-eyed boaters might also see a kingfisher.

Middlewich gives crews navigating the Cheshire Ring anti-clock-wise from Manchester their first chance of some real lock work. They will probably be glad of the exercise and they'll certainly need the practice, for there are 35 locks ahead – 5 of them through the town itself – before they reach the junction with the Macclesfield Canal. The first of these is the Middlewich Big Lock, wide gauge with a rise of 5 ft 1 in (155 cm). Right beside it is a pub, called, appropriately enough, the Big Lock. Soon after the Big Lock is a series of three narrow locks, very close together with a total rise of nearly 33 ft (10 m).

A lively place with good shops and pubs, Middlewich is a canal town to the core. There are three boatyards, good moorings and a branch of the Shropshire Union Canal which strikes off on a south-westerly course to connect with its main line at Barbridge. There are two watering points – one near the Big Lock, the other just beyond the bridge marking the start of the Middlewich Branch of the 'Shroppie' – and souvenir hunters will no doubt be happy to browse through the canal shop run by Middlewich Narrow Boats, reached soon after passing through the top lock of the rise of three. Accommodating to the last, the town provides another handy pub at King's Lock, the town's southern canal gateway.

From now on the canal provides increasing opportunities for the crew to get in trim, though at first the course is relatively easy over more ground affected by salt-mining operations. At Wheelock, near the ancient market town of Sandbach, are the first of a number of narrow gauge locks set in pairs. Not all of them are in operation, but in several places the skipper will have a choice of which lock to use. The Wheelock flight of eight locks takes you up nearly 80 ft (24 m) to the village of Hassall Green. Beyond Rode Heath – where there is the unusual Thurlwood Steel Lock, built in 1957 in an attempt to counteract subsidence – a further 11 locks climb the ascent poignantly labelled 'Heartbreak Hill', near the top of which the Trent and Mersey is crossed by the Red Bull Aqueduct carrying the Macclesfield Canal at the start of its journey northwards. The final lock opens into Harding's Wood Junction at Kidsgrove, Staffordshire.

Kidsgrove is well worth a stop for canal buffs. Its early development as a centre for the production of coal and iron was greatly helped by the Trent and Mersey. South of Harding's Wood Junction, just beyond the town's railway station, is the mouth of Harecastle Tunnel, taking the canal a distance of 2,919 yds (2,627 m) through Harecastle Hill. Built by Thomas Telford and completed in 1827, it is the second canal tunnel to be cut through the hill. The first, opened in 1777, was the work of James Brindley who is buried in Kidsgrove.

Macclesfield Canal

Delightful throughout its length of nearly 28 miles (45 km), the Macclesfield Canal actually passes through the old silk town and on to Marple, where it joins the Peak Forest Canal, 500 ft (150 m) above sea level and overlooked by Pennine grandeur. No one is likely to be disappointed by the scenery anywhere along the canal's course. It is relatively easy to navigate – only 12 locks in a flight at Bosley plus the stop lock just outside Kidsgrove. The Bosley flight is some 11 miles (18 km) along the route – three or four hours' cruising if you don't stop along the way – so crews will be able to relax after toiling from Middlewich, although the odd swing bridge will help to keep them in trim.

Stone 'roving' bridges, which allowed the horses towing boats to cross from one side of the canal to the other, are a picturesque feature of the waterway.

The Macclesfield was built to serve the mills and factories of Cheshire and what is now Greater Manchester so there is plenty to see for those interested in industrial architecture. It was opened in 1831, at a time when people were beginning to think railways rather than canals. But it managed to compete effectively – perhaps because it was owned for much of the time by a railway company.

Beyond the stop lock at Kent Green, the canal reaches open countryside dominated by Mow Cop, towering 1,100 ft (330 m) above sea level and capped by an eighteenth-century folly. A little further north, on the canal's western side, is Little Moreton Hall, one of the country's most perfect examples of a moated, black-and-white timbered house, built in the mid-sixteenth century and now owned by the National Trust. At Congleton, 6 canal miles (10 km) from Harding's Wood Junction, it might be prudent to re-stock the galley, since there are few places offering much in the way of shops until Macclesfield, a good 10 miles (16 km) further north.

Beyond Congleton the canal curves first to the west and then eastwards around the foot of The Cloud, a 1,000 ft (300 m) high fell whose presence heralds the approaching flight of locks. In the next mile or so boats ascend almost 120 ft (36 m) to an altitude of some 500 ft (150 m) above sea level, the highest stretch of waterway in England. Crew members will have the satisfaction of knowing they are working in one of the country's most spectacular canal settings as they labour up the flight. For good measure, there are a couple of hefty swing bridges to be shifted as the canal pursues its way towards **Macclesfield**.

A town of cobbled streets with a medieval marketplace and grand buildings of the Industrial Revolution, Macclesfield has shops galore and 65 pubs selling real ale. It also has a Working Silk Museum – the town still has an important textile industry – and a Sunday School Heritage Centre. The canal soars above and beyond Macclesfield, crossing a 60 ft (18 m) embankment and two aqueducts to reach Bollington, a mill town on the edge of the Peak District National Park and surrounded, not unexpectedly, by hills. Much of the remaining 8 miles (13 km) or so of the Macclesfield pass through sparsely populated, peaceful upland country, and at its junction with the Peak Forest Canal, in Marple, the canal ends in a pleasing waterside setting.

Peak Forest Canal

Completed in 1800 to serve the Pennine limestone quarries, the waterway is in two sections: the Upper Peak Forest, trailing 6½ miles (10.4 km) southwards to Whaley Bridge and Buxworth, and the Lower Peak Forest which sets off towards Manchester, tumbling dramatically over 16 locks in its first mile. Both parts cross countryside of great beauty.

The upper section may seem like a diversion from the main route of the Cheshire Ring, but skippers should allow time to make the trip to Whaley Bridge, for it really is worth while. For the first half of its distance the canal winds precariously across rugged Peak District countryside softened by woodland, high above the valley of the River Goyt. The views are stupendous. There are no locks to negotiate on the journey to Whaley Bridge, but there are three lift bridges and a couple to be swung.

Beyond the typically Pennine town of New Mills, on the Cheshire–Derbyshire border, the waterway becomes rather shallow, and helmsmen would be wise to keep to the centre of the channel. Not far from its terminus, the canal divides. The left-hand arm leads into Buxworth Basin, once bustling with activity as cargoes of limestone were loaded from boats and wagons of the Peak Forest Tramway which led from the quarries at Doveholes, some 6 miles (10 km) away. The basin is now undergoing restoration. At **Whaley Bridge** the Upper Peak Forest ends in a tranquil basin and slides into the doorway of a building in which goods were transferred to trains on the Cromford and High Peak Railway. Built in 1832, the old dock is now used by a boat hire company.

The Lower Peak Forest Canal gets off to a good start as it leaves Marple, descending 214 ft (64 m) over 16 locks before crossing 100 ft (30 m) above the wooded gorge of the River Goyt on an impressive aqueduct twinned with an even more awesome railway viaduct. For the next 4 miles (6 km) or so the countryside continues to be pleasantly rural, and the canal passes through two tunnels, Hyde Bank Tunnel, 308 yds (277 m) long, near Romiley, and Woodley Tunnel, 176 yds (158 m), near Bredbury. Gradually, though, the scenery becomes more urban, if not downright industrial, as the Mancunian outposts of Hyde and Dukinfield are approached. At Dukinfield boats take a sharp left turn and enter the final stages in their circuit of the Cheshire Ring.

Ashton and Rochdale Canals

The next, and last, 7 miles (11 km) take boats through the areas of Ashton under-Tyne, Droylsden and Openshaw, places as much a part of the Industrial Revolution as the canals themselves. There is little to stir the soul along this stretch, except perhaps for those whose sense of history allows them to see beauty in the broken windows, grimy brickwork and rusting pipes of old factories. But there is plenty to do to keep depression at bay: 18 locks on the Ashton Canal, between Fairfield and Ducie Street junctions, then another 9 on the final one-mile stretch of the Rochdale Canal. It can be hard and frustrating work, too, for many of the locks are in a poor state of repair, with leaking paddles and badly fitting gates. One thing is certain: after reaching Castlefield to complete the 102-mile (163 km) round trip, no one in the crew is likely to have a sleepless night.

Addresses

General information

Manchester Ship Canal Co.,
Dock Office,
Trafford Road,
Manchester M5 2CB
Tel: 061 872 2411

North West Tourist Board (provides information on tourist attractions in Cheshire, Greater Manchester, Lancashire, Merseyside, and Derbyshire's High Peak District)
The Last Drop Village,
Bromley Cross,
Bolton BL7 9PZ
Tel: 0204 591511

Bridgewater Canal (Main Line)

Brochures/reservations

Brinks Boats,
The Old Boatyard,
Worsley,
Manchester M28 4WN
Tel: 061 728 1184

Claymoore Navigation Ltd,
The Wharf,
Preston Brook,
Warrington,
Cheshire WA4 4BA
Tel: 0928 717273

Egerton Narrow Boats Ltd,
The Old Boat Yard,
Worsley,
Manchester M28 4WN
Tel: 061 793 7031

Trent and Mersey Canal

Brochures/reservations

Anderson Boats,
Wych House Lane,
Middlewich,
Cheshire CW10 9BQ
Tel: 060684 3668

Black Prince Holidays Ltd (base near Northwich)
Stoke Prior,
Bromsgrove,
Worcestershire B60 4LA
Tel: 0527 575115

Clare Cruisers Ltd,
Uplands Basin,
Uplands Road,
Anderton,
Northwich,
Cheshire CW9 6AJ
Tel: 0606 77199

Colliery Narrow Boat Co. Ltd,
Wincham Wharf,
220 Manchester Road,
Lostock Gralam,
Cheshire CW9 7NT
Tel: 0606 44672

IML Waterway Cruising Ltd (base at Anderton Marina)
Bank Newton,
Gargrave,
Skipton,
North Yorkshire BD23 3NT
Tel: 0756 749492

Middlewich Narrowboats,
Canal Terrace,
Middlewich,
Cheshire CW10 9BD
Tel: 060684 2460

Macclesfield Canal

Brochures/reservations

Constellation Cruisers,
Lyme Road,
Higher Poynton,
Stockport,
Cheshire SK12 1TH
Tel: 0625 873471

Heritage Boats (base at Kent Green)
Scholar Green,
Stoke-on-Trent ST7 3JZ
Tel: 07816 5700

Peak Forest Cruisers,
The Wharf,
Buxton Road,
Macclesfield,
Cheshire SK10 1LZ
Tel: 0625 24172.

David Piper,
Red Bull Basin,
Church Lawton,
Stoke-on-Trent ST7 3AJ
Tel: 07816 4754

Peak Forest, Ashton and Rochdale Canals

Brochures/reservations

Russwell Canal Boats Ltd,
7 Prince's Drive,
Marple,
Cheshire SK6 6NJ
Tel: 061 427 5121

Unicorn Marine,
Canal Wharf,
Whaley Bridge,
Cheshire SK12 7LS
Tel: 06633 3411

WALES

A pair of hotel boats 'breasted up' to save mooring space at a pub on the Llangollen Canal

The topography of Wales, of course, means that it could never be much of a country for navigable waterways. A few canals were cut, short ones, and mainly from the coast, a short way up valleys to bring coal down. But three fairly lengthy ones were constructed, two of which are still in use throughout their length. One of these, the Llangollen, is said to be the most popular waterway in the United Kingdom.

Llangollen Canal

This most attractive waterway begins at Hurleston Junction, about a mile south of Barbridge, where a right-angled turn from the Shropshire Union, leads straight into the first of a flight of four locks. On the towpath is a notice warning that boats with a draught of more than 2 ft (0.6 m) should proceed at their own risk, although many boats drawing 2 ft 6 in (0.75 m) and more manage to make it all the way to Llangollen. Another point to take into account is the fact that there is a current of about 1 mph (1.6 kph) running against you. It will make quite a difference on your return journey timings.

The locks immediately take boats into the tranquil rural countryside of the Cheshire–Shropshire borderlands. One soon appreciates why the Llangollen is said to be the most popular waterway in the United Kingdom, with up to 400 boats a week passing along its length during the summer peak. More locks – two at Swanley and three at Baddiley – lead to the attractive village of **Wrenbury** where the former mill now serves as offices and canal shop of English County Cruisers, which offers a high standard of hire craft. An old-fashioned wooden lift bridge which would look more familiar in a Dutch landscape carries road traffic across the canal. Use your windlass to lift it.

Marbury Lock is a pleasant alternative mooring to Wrenbury, which can get rather busy. **Marbury** itself is about three-quarters of a mile (1.2 km) from the canal, but is worth a visit. There is a very pretty church on the edge of Big Mere, first of the many Shropshire meres along the waterway, and an attractive old pub, The Swan. Much of the land in this parish belongs to the Crown. At Grindley Brook there is a flight of six locks, three of which form a staircase. The lock keeper is usually present to help boats through. There is a shop near the locks.

Whitchurch – we are now in Shropshire – is a splendid old town with narrow, gently winding streets. It is perhaps a twenty-five

Lift bridge at Wrenbury (Llangollen Canal)

minute walk from the canal, but worth the effort. Viking Afloat, another boatyard offering quality narrow boats for hire, has a base nearby. Another well-known hire boat company, Black Prince, has a marina at the end of the old Prees Branch on the far side of **Whixall Moss**. The branch once served nearby clay pits which provided material to repair the canal. Whixall Moss is a large area of peat bog, holding great appeal for botanists and entomologists. For a short time along this stretch the canal is actually in Wales as the border winds around. At the quiet village of Bettisfield we are in the Welsh county of Clwyd. At Welshampton, a mile or so along the waterway, we are back in Shropshire.

Beyond Welshampton the canal passes two lakes, Cole Mere and Blake Mere. The towpath runs along the edge of Blake Mere, an unspoilt lake with abundant birdlife, including grebe. At the far end of the lake the canal enters the 87 yd (78 m) Ellesmere Tunnel, emerging in open parkland. **Ellesmere** is a pleasant old market town, reached by a small arm along which are some good moorings. The last two of the Llangollen's 21 locks are reached at New Marton, where there is also a shop with an off-licence and a working pottery. The Welsh Hills are closing in.

At Chirk the waterway enters Wales once and for all as it crosses the River Ceiriog on an impressive aqueduct flanked by an even more impressive railway viaduct. At the far end it passes through a short tunnel to emerge in scenery which becomes increasingly stupendous. And so to the renowned **Pontcysyllte Aqueduct**, 1,000 ft (300 m) long and soaring 120 ft (36 m) above the River Dee. The work of canal engineer Thomas Telford, the aqueduct is a cast-iron trough set on stone piers. It was completed in 1805. The sight of boats traversing this elegant construction is as amazing now as it was then. The view from the aqueduct is no less awesome – especially from the unguarded side opposite the towpath – though it is a pity that one of the more dominant features of the landscape below is a sewage works.

Across the aqueduct, at Trevor wharf, the canal makes a sudden right-angle turn into the narrow, shallow final stretch to **Llangollen**, where there are good moorings. There are others at the pub near Sun Trevor Bridge. It's about a mile out of town but worth it if the moorings there are crowded and you don't mind a gentle stroll along the towpath.

Famous for its annual International Eisteddfod, Llangollen is dominated by the ruins of Castell Dinas Bran, standing on a 1,100 ft (330 m) hill. The former castle home of a Prince of Powys, it served as a fortress against English invaders. It is a steep climb to the summit, but the views are rewarding. In the town a 600-year-old stone bridge crosses the River Dee and leads to the main street.

The Vale of Llangollen offers a great deal to those who enjoy such outdoor activities as walking, climbing, pony trekking and canoeing. There are horse-drawn boat trips and steam train rides to Horseshoe Falls, Telford's weir which draws water from the Dee to feed the canal.

Monmouthshire and Brecon Canal

Isolated from the rest of the waterway system, the 'Mon and Brec' covers a distance of just over 33 miles (53 km) from Pontypool to Brecon and its six locks raise it a total of 60 ft (18 m). It may seem like the kind of canal you can cover in a couple of days, but in fact it is one to tarry on. Enthusiasts claim it is the most scenic canal in England and Wales – almost its entire length is in the beautiful Brecon Beacons National Park.

The Mon and Brec owes its survival to the national park. Like many waterways abandoned by commercial users, it soon fell into a state of bad repair, and the lower section – the original Monmouthshire Canal that flowed from Pontypool to Newport – has probably been lost for good since parts of it have been filled in. The present line, the old Brecknock and Abergavenny Canal, was saved when those planning the park's development realised the waterway's immense value as a complementary amenity. Restoration work began in 1964 and was completed in 1970.

The **Brecon Beacons National Park** covers some 520 sq. miles (1,347 sq. km) of largely mountainous countryside, and the canal gives holidaymakers a chance to enjoy it from an unusual viewpoint. Footways and bridle paths link up with the towpath in many places so exploration can easily be extended beyond the water's edge. The park contains a forest reserve and three nature reserves and there are opportunities for bird-watching and wildlife-spotting as well as such pursuits as sailing, caving and pony-trekking. Nature-lovers will find much to interest them on the canal itself, with a wide variety of aquatic plants and insect life, reeds and plantains. There are many kinds of tree to identify – among the alders lining each bank are oak and ash, sycamore and wild cherry. – and for bird-watchers a wealth of water-related species.

For all practical purposes, navigation on the Mon and Brec begins in the Pontymoile Basin at **Pontypool**. Below there navigation is possible, but difficult. Pontypool, an ancient industrial town which has always maintained its rural links, is soon left behind as the canal heads north on a course of twists and turns that present an ever-changing view. Although there are few settlements directly on the waterside in the early reaches, one never has far to go find a shop or pub. Goytre Wharf, 6 miles (9.6 km) from Pontypool, has an appealing woodland setting, and old lime kilns provide evidence of its past activity.

Upstream from Goytre, the countryside becomes ever steeper, but the Mon and Brec manages to maintain a level course, weaving into horseshoe bends and crossing streams and sudden changes of level on stone aqueducts. The substantial but attractive town of **Abergavenny**, with its long, handsome main street and ruined eleventh-century castle, is about a mile from the canal, but boats can be moored at Llanfoist. Abergavenny, on the banks of the River Usk and set against a superb mountainous backdrop, is worth the walk or bus trip. From Llanfoist Wharf you can trace on foot the line of one of the many old tramways which once transported raw material to the canal from nearby iron works and collieries.

The Usk moves closer as the canal continues northwards past Govilon, Gilwern and Glangrwyney. From the village of Llangattock, a medieval bridge with 13 arches crosses the Usk to the elegant market town of Crickhowell, a centre for rugged outdoor holidays, such as caving and rock-climbing in the surrounding hills. About 5 miles (8 km) beyond Llangattock Wharf, after passing through the thickly wooded Glen Usk Park, the canal reaches the first of the Llangynidr flight of five locks which lift the Mon and Brec 50 ft (15 m) – its first change of level in 23 miles (37 km). Before tackling the second lock, just round the corner beyond the next bridge, the crew might like to refresh themselves at the Coach and Horses pub at Cwm Crawnon. The remaining three locks of the flight are in a glorious woodland setting. The convention on the Mon and Brec is to leave lock chambers empty with the bottom gates open.

As the upper Usk Valley narrows, river and canal huddle ever closer together, with the Mon and Brec high above the Usk. The woodland begins to open out into pastures as the 375 yd (338 m) Ashford Tunnel is approached. Talybont, reached soon after the tunnel, is an attractive holiday village for hikers, anglers and riders. It has three canalside pubs. Llangorse Lake, about 3 miles (5 km) north of the village, cover 500 acres (202 hectares) and is the largest natural stretch of water in South Wales. There are good facilities for water sports and wildlife is found in abundance.

The canal approaches **Brecon** as snakily restless as it left Pontypool. Brynich Lock lifts it the final 10 ft (3 m) and the course straightens into the old city, passing attractive waterfront houses. A popular tourist centre, Brecon has a cathedral which was originally a thirteenth-century priory, an eleventh-century castle, two museums and plenty of pubs and restaurants.

Addresses

General information

The Wales Centre,
24 Piccadilly,
London W1V 9PB
Tel: 01-409 0969

Wales Tourist Board,
North Wales Regional Office,
77 Conway Road,
Colwyn Bay,
Clwyd LL29 7LN
Tel: 0492 31731

Llangollen Canal

Brochures/reservations

Anglo Welsh Waterways Holidays (base at Trevor)
Canal Basin,
Leicester Road,
Market Harborough,
Leics LE16 7BJ
Tel: 0858 66910

Black Prince Holidays (base on Prees Branch)
The Wharf,
Hanbury Road,
Stoke Prior,
Bromsgrove,
Worcestershire B60 4LA
Tel: 0527 575115

Ellesmere Boats,
Lloran House,
53 Watergate Street,
Ellesmere,
Shropshire SY12 0EX
Tel: 069171 2610

English County Cruisers,
Wrenbury Mill,
Near Nantwich,
Cheshire CW5 8HG
Tel: 0270 780544

Viking Afloat Ltd (base at Whitchurch)
Lowersmoor Wharf,
Lowersmoor Terrace,
Worcester WR1 2RX
Tel: 0905 612707 or 28667/8

Monmouthshire and Brecon Canal

General information

Wales Tourist Board,
South Wales Regional Office,
Ty Croeso,
6 Gloucester Place,
Swansea SA1 1TY
Tel: 0792 465204

Brochures/reservations

Beacon Park Boats,
Llangattock Park House,
Llangattock,
Crickhowell,
Powys NP8 1LD
Tel: 0873 810240

Castle Narrowboats,
Church Road Wharf,
Gilwern,
Abergavenny,
Gwent NP7 0EP
Tel: 0873 830001

Country Crafts Boat Hire,
Oaklands Lodge,
Llanddow,

Near Brecon,
Powys LD3 9TD
Tel: 0874 2880

Red Line Boats,
Goytre Wharf,
Llanover,
Abergavenny,
Gwent NP7 9EW
Tel: 0873 880516

Road House Holiday Hire Narrow Boats,
The Road House,
Main Road,
Gilwern,
Gwent NP7 0AS
Tel: 0873 830240

WATERLUDE: BOAT HOTELIERS

Chris and Andy Newman

Nobody who knows Chris and Andy Newman would be surprised to learn that their wedding reception was held aboard four narrow boats, followed by a free-for-all at a canalside pub for 'half the cut'. Their hotel boats, operated as the Charter Cruising Company, Rugby, cover nearly thirty routes in England and Wales, and business now attracts a high proportion of repeat bookings.

'Our regular customer ratio is 70 per cent,' says Chris. 'That's why we are so keen to maintain standards, to provide good professional crews and to introduce new routes into the brochure regularly.'

Their combined talents and their love and knowledge of the waterways have contributed to their success in a small but highly competitive sector of the leisure industry. They are the first to admit that several strokes of luck have also played an important part.

Although she grew up in Hertfordshire – very much a waterways county – Chris had no real connection with the canals until she took a job in the head office accounts department of a motor sales group and met Andy, who was working as manager of the company's St Albans branch.

'I saw him on Friday mornings when he called for petty cash, and one day he asked me out. That was in 1974. He happened to be living on a boat. We carried on with ordinary office jobs for the next two years until the boat was paid for.'

Chris's first job had been as a secretary at British Aerospace. 'I could see myself falling into the inevitable semi on an estate with 2.8 children, and I made up my mind I wasn't going to do this,' she says.

She 'bluffed' her way into a hotel receptionist's job in Devon, enjoying a busy social life, and stayed there for four years – an experience which, with her accounting and secretarial skills, she acknowledges, helped equip her for the work she does now.

Andy was born and bred beside the southern Grand Union Canal. One of his best school friends was the son of a lock keeper, and the canal bank was his playground. Early in his working life, Andy made a move which set him on the first, crucial rung of his career ladder. He took a job which provided a company car. This meant selling his nearly new MGB sports car which provided the money to get him afloat for the first time.

By the time he and Chris met, he had a 53 ft (16 m) narrow boat, *Aries*, built for him by Braunston Boats. 'I paid £3,980 for it, fully fitted, in 1971,' says Andy. 'Five years later I sold it in pristine condition for £8,000.'

Now he and Chris could afford to indulge in a job which did not have a good salary attached. They upped stakes and joined the crew of a pair of hotel boats. The company, Inland Navigators, was operated by Peter Frowd and his wife Shirley for thirty years until Peter's death in the late 1980s. It is now run by another couple.

'Peter was almost the founding father of modern hotel boating,' says Andy. 'He's certainly introduced more people to hotel boating than anyone else.'

Chris recalls her first experience of cooking for hotel boat guests as 'an absolute disaster'.

'I was too ambitious,' she says. 'It was a simple enough meal – roast beef. By 7 pm it should all have been ready. But it got to seven o'clock and I'd forgotten to make the gravy, and the sweet had taken hours to prepare. I just died. I went to have a shower and bawled my eyes out. After that, things got better . . . I think!'

The next career milestone was setting up a company in 1978, running their own craft as a charter boat – hence the name Charter Cruising. This was the 70 ft (21 m) narrow boat *Vixen*, one of the four on which they held their wedding reception. *Vixen* was their home for four years. It had six berths for guests, and two more were fitted later. But the bookings didn't exactly flow in.

Chris explains: 'It was fun, but it never made any money. There wasn't really a market for whole-boat charters. It was an oil and water situation – a mixture of hire boat and hotel boat customers. If we had a party of six people they wanted to steer the boat themselves, and if there were just one or two chartering it, it was too expensive to run.'

Fortunately, between trips, and in winter, she was able to work in a canalside pub and restaurant, and Andy, a trained engineer, sub-contracted his labour to a nearby boat company. For a time they ran *Vixen* as a restaurant boat. The crunch came at the end of 1981. With his daytime job and the restaurant boat, Andy's working day was from 9 am until midnight. Chris spent all day cooking and worked on the restaurant boat at night.

'It was just too much, though the struggle to survive was good experience,' Andy reminisces.

Chris went to France for a few weeks to work on a hotel barge run by friends. Andy, meanwhile, had been to see a canal boatyard which he had heard was available between Worcester and the River Severn. Chris returned from France with her mind full of hotel boating, took one look at the boatyard and hated it.

'It would have meant selling *Vixen* and living in a flat above the boatyard. I thought it was awful. I said I wanted to do hotel boating,' says Chris.

Andy knew of someone who was giving up hotel boats to run horse-drawn trip boats. He arranged a visit to see a motor boat and butty called *Tsarina* and *Tsarevna*.

'Driving there,' says Chris, 'I told Andy that we were not going to buy the butty – just the motor boat. We didn't know how much the owner wanted for the boats, anyway. When we saw the butty, *Tsarevna*, I just fell in love with it. She was very sad, but we could see the potential.'

'The butty had been laid-up for two years. It had just festered,' says Andy. 'We had a buyer lined up for *Vixen*, someone who wouldn't look at any other boat.'

So *Tsarina* and *Tsarevna*, graciously liveried in maroon and cream, became Charter Cruising Company's first hotel boats. For the first season – 1982 – only the motor boat was used – the butty needed a lot of attention. In the following seasons the boats were run extensively as a pair, initially crewed by Chris and Andy themselves, and hundreds of people from many parts of the world spent holidays aboard them.

Then Chris and Andy became parents.

'Sarah was six weeks old when the season started, and she was no bother,' says Chris. 'We took on an extra crew member and it worked perfectly, but we knew that when Sarah got a little older we wouldn't be able to run the boats ourselves. We were thinking about what to do next. In our usual way, we weren't really making definite plans, but something cropped up.'

They heard by chance that Willow Wren Hotel Cruises, a well-known company at Rugby was on the market. Chris and Andy, away on the cut, but without passengers, moved fast, made phone calls and hired a car to get them back to base. They had a meeting with the seller, a deal was made to buy the wharf, office and two pairs of boats. Everything was arranged – even the finance – then at the last minute the bank changed its mind. The couple did the rounds of the other banks, but it seemed that all was lost – until a colleague of Andy's in the Association of Pleasure Cruising Operators said: 'Forget the banks. Go to the finance houses. Get it on HP.' He suggested a company and the person to contact.

'It turned out to be an old friend of mine from way back. I'd lost touch with him. We couldn't believe it,' says Andy. 'He listened and said yes. It was obvious we were destined to have it.'

There was a slight shortfall in the sum available, but the vendor let them pay the balance monthly, interest-free.

Chris and Andy appreciate the 'fairy godparents' who have enabled them to achieve their ambition – and their parents who have constantly encouraged them in their chosen lifestyle.

When Chris's mother had some money to invest, she bought a wide-beamed boat, *Tranquil Rose*, which cruises the Thames as a hotel boat.

Charter Cruising Company has a lot of repeat business, so new routes are regularly introduced. Lasting friendships are made. Guests swop addresses and arrange to meet up on future cruises.

'We get Australians, New Zealanders, Americans and Canadians, as well as people from the UK,' says Andy. 'Some of our guests are 75 to 80 years old, some are young. A lot of them are travelling alone, especially the New Zealanders. We get single women – career women – teachers, solicitors, doctors. Guests can be as active as they like, helping with the locks, taking a walk on the towpath, or they can just sit back and relax.

'The Americans are not usually particularly wealthy people – those tend to go on the French hotel barges. We get more of the newly retired couples dipping into their life savings – the pioneer Americans. We get some very interesting people.

'Some of the overseas visitors wouldn't go into a pub on their own – they wouldn't know the rules of the game. But they enjoy going in with the crew. They love watching the locals play skittles or darts. They ask if they should tip the barmaid. They try half a pint of bitter – they drink in the atmosphere rather than the beer.'

Running hotel boats isn't easy, and it's not a business in which fortunes are amassed. Bookings can be affected by the exchange rate, the weather – and the Chancellor of the Exchequer.

While the clients cruise gently through the countryside, life is a whirl of activity for Chris and Andy. They stock up at the cash and carry store and drive hundreds of miles – one perhaps to Wigan, the other to Windsor, one to Chester, the other to, say, Gloucester – wherever the supplies and fresh linen have to be delivered on the waterways.

In winter the travelling stops, but bookings are made, crews for the following year have to be appointed – many work season after season on different routes, building up an intimate knowledge of the waterways. Boats have to be refitted and repainted.

'It's hard work, but we're doing what we've always wanted to do,' say the Newmans.

THE MIDLANDS

A trip boat sets off from Gas Street Basin, Birmingham

Birmingham

Cruising into the heart of Birmingham in the years immediately after World War II could hardly have been pleasurable. Interesting, perhaps. Among the remaining commercial boats carrying goods between London and the West Midlands, leisure boaters were a rare species – pioneers, in their way. Many of them were also visionaries. They could see how the waterways system could be cleaned up and generally improved for pleasure cruising at a time when the writing was clearly on the wall for the canal carrying companies, and once vital waterways were declining alarmingly into shallow, muck-ridden rubbish tips.

These people spotlighted such areas and helped to keep them open by holding rallies in frankly sordid places like Birmingham's Gas Street Basin, then surrounded by factories and warehouses. The air they breathed wasn't the most heady and clear. Indeed, if they sat on deck with a cup of tea they had to gulp it down fast to prevent it being peppered with sooty specks. At that time there was a big traffic in coal, which disappeared totally in the late 1960s.

Today, gongoozlers – the traditional name for those amiable souls who cannot resist watching the canal scene from bridge or towpath – are rewarded by a splendid, colourful view of a scrubbed-clean urban landscape and waterscape not far from New Street Station. If you find yourself in Birmingham on a business or shopping trip, it's worth taking time out to explore the inner city waterways on foot, maybe with the aim of getting afloat in the area some time.

Canal Walkabout

Birmingham no longer turns its back on the water. A 6-mile (10 km) walkway has been established alongside the Birmingham and Fazeley Canal and descriptive leaflets are available so you can identify what you are seeing. The leaflets relate to seven specific routes within the city centre waterway system, built more than 220 years ago by leading figures in canal engineering, including Thomas Telford, who tended to tunnel through, and James Brindley, who followed the contour lines. Routes covered by the walks are from Gas Street Basin to Aston Junction, Galton Valley, Warwick Bar, Salford Junction and Bournville, and from Warwick Bar to Acocks Green and Salford Junction.

Those interested in a more in-depth study of the city canal system – and Birmingham's history – can take a guided tour, in which they will learn of the Farmers Bridge flight of 13 locks that provided some interesting boating two centuries ago, and still does. It is a steep flight, most of the locks pretty close together, and it lifts boats more than 80 ft (24 m) from the Birmingham and Fazeley, built by John Smeaton and finished in 1789, to Farmers Bridge Junction and Gas Street Basin.

The guided walk underlines the way the city has preserved its industrial heritage. It starts at the basin, goes by way of the £125 million International Convention Centre scheduled for completion in the early 1990s, and takes in the much-acclaimed Museum of Science and Industry. Close by the museum, at Newhall Bridge, is a gongoozler's dream – a public viewing point from which boats passing through the Farmers Bridge flight of locks can be watched.

Due to open in 1991 on a 60-acre (24 hectare) waterside site, are a National Indoor Sports Arena, a National Aquarium, a 24-storey InterContinental Hotel, a Heritage Centre and shopping complex, all designed with the canal system as a focal point. A new pub at the Gas Street Basin is named the James Brindley, and the Georgian-style buildings in the vicinity are included in the refurbishment programme. Traditional narrow boats moored in the basin are the permanent homes of a community which is an attraction in itself.

The Birmingham Inner City Partnership, an amalgamation of local authorities, British Waterways Board and central government, has been responsible for the Cinderella story in which Gas Street Basin stars in terms of urban development. Far from being the down-at-heel, ragged-skirted unsavoury old character so well remembered by many residents and boating visitors, the revitalised basin is now an attraction in its own right.

The Partnership has set a splendid example in recognising the recreational potential of the waterways and taking appropriate action. Locks, bridges and towpaths have been restored. People set up easels and capture the relaxed ambiance of the city's new attraction. Others use cameras with the same idea in mind. Joggers pound along the towpath. Wildlife watchers find something of interest, and the gongoozler comes into his own.

Birmingham Canal Navigations

Birmingham reckons to have a bigger canal system than Venice. The network of the Birmingham Canal Navigations (BCN) consists of more than 100 miles (160 km) of waterway, with canals branching out in all directions. At one time, the canals of the BCN extended to around 160 miles (256 km). Certainly, Birmingham is the hub of the system in England and Wales.

Formed by a group of Black Country industrialists, the BCN was built between the mid eighteenth and nineteenth centuries to serve the coalmining and mineral-working industries. Carrying coal by canal instead of road when the Birmingham Canal opened in 1772 meant an instant halving of the price of coal. Although the railways took over much of the long-distance freight-carrying business in the mid nineteenth century, the BCN still had an active part to play, serving local factories. New basins were built for goods to be transferred between rail and water. The last major BCN expansion was the Cannock Extension Canal, nearly 6 miles (10 km) long and built between 1858 and 1863 to carry coal from Cannock Chase to the industries of the Black Country.

Boating on the Birmingham Canal Navigation

In the 1950s, freight tonnages on the BCN dwindled to a non-viable state, and the network was at an all-time low. However, in a situation like that the only way is up. After a few years of stagnation the fast-growing leisure business got to work on the BCN. Derelict buildings were replaced. Others were cleaned up and renovated. The blast furnaces and foundries, the forges and factories of the Black Country disappeared. Greenery returned, and the canal water improved in quality to such an extent that fish could again survive in it, which meant that anglers, too, returned. Canoeists, boating people, students of canal architecture, wildlife watchers, photographers and artists can now enjoy the pleasure of the navigation.

Strolling beside those canals can be relaxing, with a lot to see. Sometimes it can be exciting, with not a lot to see – as in the **Netherton Tunnel**. Unlike many tunnels, the Netherton has a path – one on each side, in fact. This is the place to cool off on a scorching hot summer's day. The wide tunnel is 1¾ miles (2.8 km) long, and apart from the odd shaft of light sliding down from an air vent, it is dark, moist and spooky. Great fun!

Netherton Tunnel is on a branch of the Dudley No. 2 Canal, leading northwards to the Birmingham Canal Main Line. Before you reach it there's a fine view of Netherton Hill, on the top of which stands St Andrew's Church. Here are the communal graves of cholera victims. Nails and chains were products of the area in bygone days. Half a mile from Bishtons Bridge at Netherton is the Old Swan, a renowned pub with its own real ale brewery. Some know it as 'Ma Pardoe's'. Nearby is Cobbs Engine House, a pumping station to remove water from local mines.

Dudley Tunnel is an entertainment in its own right. It is more than 3,000 yds (2,700 m) long, but without a towpath, which meant that before engines were developed boats had to be 'legged' through, crew members lying on their backs on the boat and 'walking' along the tunnel walls. The Dudley Canal Trust has carried out restoration work and built the first battery-powered narrow boat, the *Electra* in 1975 so that fume-free trips can be taken into the network of mines, natural caverns, canal basins and branches serving mines and quarries, under Dudley's Castle Hill. Other electrically powered boats have been added to the fleet, and trips into the tunnel are a major tourist attraction. The limestone mines hewn out of solid rock in the eighteenth century were a tremendous engineering achievement. Today, the latest computer technology enables us to follow the caverns' history, from the laying down of limestone 400 million years ago to the present day. This is the Singing Cavern Experience, an audio-visual show opened in 1986 by the Earl of Dudley. Internal combustion engines are banned from the tunnel.

Another big attraction today is the Black Country Museum, a re-created nineteenth-century village on 26 acres (11 hectares), in which the region's industrial heritage is depicted.

Original buildings have been reconstructed, including workers' homes, shops and the Bottle and Glass pub (licensed to sell beer). There are lime kilns by the canal, and narrow boats at their moorings. Demonstrators in costume chat to visitors about their crafts – nail making, chain making, ironworking, boat building ... Some of the products can be bought in the gift shop. Like any community, the museum is constantly developing, with new exhibits.

Behind the enterprise – and behind many others in the region – is the Black Country Tourism Initiative, set up by the local authorities of Dudley, Wolverhampton, Sandwell and Walsall, with the Heart of England Tourist Board. Still dominated by industry, the Black Country recognised its industrial heritage as a tourism attraction, of which canals are a focal point.

There are twelve locks on the Dudley No. 1 Canal, which was completed in 1792. It joins the Stourbridge Canal at the bottom of the Delph Locks flight near Brierley Hill. While the Stourbridge Canal (not part of the BCN) flourished and remained independent until nationalisation of the waterways in 1948, the Dudley Canal incurred frequent expenditure because of subsidence caused by mine workings. Nine Locks Bridge spans the canal at the flight of eight, a designated conservation area. Nine? Ah, well, because of subsidence the flight had to be completely rebuilt in 1858, and although the top and bottom locks were on the original sites, the other seven were reduced to six and re-sited to one side. A museum and information centre is housed in converted stables beside Lock No. 3. It is open to the public on special open days held by the Birmingham Canal Navigation Society.

A quarter of a mile (0.4 km) east of the bottom lock of the Delph flight is the Vine pub at Brierley Hill, known locally as the Bull and Bladder, where Daniel Batham's real ale is brewed. Across the facade of the building is a quotation from Shakespeare's *The Two Gentlemen of Verona* – 'Blessing of your heart you brew good ale.'

North of the Delph Locks, the canal skirts what was the Round Oak Steelworks, producing iron and steel for nearly two centuries. It was shut down in 1983. A little farther on is the deepest lock on the BCN, Blowers Green lock, with a 12 ft (3.6 m) rise.

Two of the BCN waterways, the Wyrley and Essington Canal (or 'Curly Wyrley') and the Walsall Branch Canal, meet at **Birchills**, where a canal museum has been set up at the Boatman's Rest. This was once a mission hall, operated by an organisation which had the spiritual welfare of the boat families at heart. Services were held and recreational facilities provided – minus alcohol. Letters were written on behalf of untutored boatmen, and their children were given the basics of an education during their occasional visits. Overnight accommodation was available for canal workers, both human and equine.

In fifty years the character of the BCN has changed enormously, and although restoration work and 'cityscaping' has made the waterways a great leisure facility, one can respect the feelings of those who feel Birmingham and the Black Country has lost its heart. There are fears, too, through much of the country as a whole, that property developers are allowed to be over-zealous in building on canalside sites, to the detriment of the historical and leisure aspects of the environment. While neat, colourful gardens are pleasant enough to cruise by, they do decrease the availability of moorings and angling spots near towns and villages, and detract from the general appeal to canal users.

Sandwell, in the Black Country, has been developing 120 canalside acres (48 hectares) as a shopping, leisure and entertainment project, with hotels and department stores. 'Sandwell 2000' is scheduled for opening in 1992. Some like the idea, some don't. While conceding that Birmingham's canal zone needed a facelift, some feel it's gone too far, with consequent loss of character, and they are uneasy at the prospect of similar developments in many other parts of the canal system.

Thanks largely to the campaigning efforts of the Inland Waterways Association, who fought the apathy of successive postwar governments for years, the waterways of the UK now form attractive – in many parts beautiful – places, on or beside which thousands can spend their leisure time. It hasn't taken long for the property developers to cast their greedy eyes on the halcyon scene nationwide and see vast profits there for the plucking. Town planners are by their nature captivated by talk of leisure complexes, hotels, upmarket housing, office towers and conference facilities because of the income such projects will generate for their town or city.

The losers are the ordinary canal addicts, loyal to their leisure haven, who see great tracts of waterside environment disappearing under concrete. These developments are escalating in many areas, and few include marinas which might constitute some slight compensation for the loss of a traditional setting. If you think this is unfair comment, consider the high streets of Britain which have lost their individuality because of developments which may look good at the planning stage and identical on completion. Developers know a good thing when they see one and are already demonstrating their expertise on making canalside towns look alike.

The campaigning spirit of conservationists will have to be much to the fore in the 1990s if the waterways in urban areas are not to lose their identity and their charm.

Trent and Mersey Canal

(Shardlow to Great Haywood)

Purists will say that the Trent and Mersey really begins at Derwent Mouth, where it meets the River Trent, but romantics will insist it starts at the first of the canal's distinctive black and white painted cast-iron mile posts – the one that says 'Preston Brook 92 Miles' and shows a blank space under the word 'Shardlow'. In this chapter we'll be travelling only as far as Great Haywood. Other parts of the waterway are dealt with in the chapters on the Cheshire and Four Counties Rings.

A favourite with canal enthusiasts, **Shardlow** is a prime example of the inland ports that thrived during the eighteenth and nineteenth centuries. The architecture of its heyday is so well preserved it might have been built within the last couple of years rather than a couple of centuries ago. The waterfront is dominated by the dignified bulk of the eighteenth-century Trent Mill, which has a large central arch, an entrance for boats unloading corn. The mill has recently been restored and is now a popular restaurant. Adjacent buildings are used by a narrow boat hire company.

The River Trent, no longer navigable, follows the canal closely as it traverses an agricultural landscape, thickly wooded in parts. The village of **Weston upon Trent** is actually separated from the river by the canal. Its main claim to fame is that it has a settlement of Ukrainians, established during World War II. Willington Power Station dominates the landscape, and for a time the canal has a railway line as a noisy neighbour. But at Willington itself there are good moorings in an attractive setting. Ancient Repton, once the capital of the kingdom of Mercia and now well known for its sixteenth-century public school, is about 1½ miles (2.4 km) away.

Between Willington and Burton upon Trent the canal passes from Derbyshire into Staffordshire, crossing the River Dove on a stone aqueduct with nine arches. Your nose alone will tell you that Burton is a major centre for the brewing of beer, and has been since the thirteenth century when the industry was started by monks at the local abbey. It's the gypsum in Burton's water that makes it such a distinctive beer. You can learn all about it in the National Brewery Museum located in the former Tiger Brewery in Anglesey Road. There's also the Bass Museum in Horninglow Street, about fifteen minutes on foot from Horninglow Basin.

Beyond Burton the Trent and Mersey follows an almost straight course, accompanied for too long by the busy A38 trunk road, and with locks spaced out just far enough to keep the crew alert. The attractive villages of Wynchnor and Alrewas are within twenty cruising minutes of Fradley Junction, where the Coventry Canal strikes off to the west.

Fradley would scarcely exist if it were not for the canals. Visitors are encouraged to leave their cars outside the village, for the only access is, virtually, the towpath. It's only a few minutes' walk and the Swan pub is conveniently placed opposite the junction of the two waterways. Fradley is a great place for gongoozling. You can sit outside the Swan for hours, watching the boats go by, listening to boat talk, talking boat talk . . . And you can drive yourself crazy reading the 'Boat For Sale' cards in the window of the village shop. For boaters there is also some work to be done: five locks lift the Trent and Mersey through Fradley.

Just before Woodend Lock the canal makes an abrupt change of direction – to the north west, a course it will more or less maintain to Preston Brook. At **Armitage**, a town distinguished worldwide for its manufacture of lavatory bowls, the canal passes through a cutting that used to be a 130 yd (120 m) tunnel until its roof was removed in 1971 because of subsidence problems. Spode House, former home of the chinaware magnate Josiah Spode, overlooks the waterway. Rugeley power station, usually spouting stark-white steam, becomes a daunting landmark, but the town makes a cheerful stop, if only to stock up from its shops and lively street market.

Screams and a ghostly figure are said to have been witnessed in the area between the town centre and Brindley Bank Aqueduct where the body of 37-year-old Mrs Christina Collins was found on a June morning in 1839. Travelling as the sole passenger on a canal boat, she had been 'most barbarously treated', as the headstone of her grave in St Augustine's Churchyard, Rugeley, puts it. The three crew men, still drunk when they were arrested shortly after the body's discovery, were charged with her murder. Two of them were subsequently hanged in public in Stafford.

Beyond Rugeley the Trent and Mersey enters a delightfully rural area and is fringed on both sides by wild flowers and rhododendrons as it reaches Great Haywood.

Caldon Canal

It's difficult to imagine, as you enter the Caldon Canal just above Etruria Top Lock, near Stoke-on-Trent that you are about to navigate one of the loveliest waterways in England, for it gets off to a sorry, rubbish-strewn start as it passes through industrial **Hanley**. However, there is the consolation of seeing three of the very few working narrow boats still in use in the United Kingdom. *Milton Maid*, *Queen* and *Princess* are used by the Potteries firm of Johnson Bros to transport tableware – cups, saucers, plates, etc. – between three canalside factories and a packing and distribution point. Each trip is only 1½ miles (2.4 km) long at most, but the firm finds that the use of waterborne transport reduces breakages significantly.

The Caldon – or the Caldon Branch of the Trent and Mersey Canal, to be strictly accurate – travels 9 miles (14 km) from Etruria to Hazelhurst Junction where it splits into two arms. The Leek Branch soars over a fine stone aqueduct to complete its journey 3½ miles (5.6 km) away in the town of Leek, while the main line continues for another 8 miles (13 km) to Froghall, whose lime kilns, now derelict, caused the canal to be opened in 1778. The Leek Branch was opened eighteen years later, and in 1811 another 13-mile (21 km) branch was completed to Uttoxeter. But the railways soon put an end to the Uttoxeter Branch. Commercial traffic ceased on the Leek arm in 1939 and on the canal as a whole in 1956. In 1974, after years of effort by the Caldon Canal Society, backed by the British Waterways Board and local authorities – to say nothing of thousands of man hours of labour contributed by volunteers – the canal was again opened to navigation.

The first of five bascule bridges leads the Caldon away from the restless streets of Hanley, but real open country isn't reached until the other side of Engine Lock, about 5½ miles (8.8 km) from the start. At Stockton Brook a flight of five locks lifts the canal to its summit level of 484 ft (145 m) above sea level. Two and a half miles (4 km) further on, just beyond the aqueduct that takes the Leek Branch over the main line, the canal begins its descent through the three Hazelhurst New Locks, built in 1842 to replace an original staircase.

Traditional costume on horse-drawn trip boat, Caldon Canal

Cheddleton, only 4 miles (6.4 km) by road from Leek, is a delightful mooring place. Here, a pair of old water mills, once used for grinding flint needed by the potteries industry, have been restored as a working museum. They stand in a most picturesque setting below the level of the canal. From Cheddleton, the Caldon enters an area of stunning beauty, running parallel with the River Churnet, which actually joins the canal at Oakameadow Ford Lock and stays with it as far as **Consall Forge**. Once the site of a great water-powered iron works, Consall Forge is now one of the most secluded places on the waterways system. The pub here, the Black Lion, can only be reached by boat or on foot. A 76 yd (68.4 m) tunnel leads to the superb setting of **Froghall Junction** where there is lots of green space for picnics. The old wharf building houses a restaurant and canal shop, and Badger, the horse who draws a trip boat between the junction and Flint Mill Lock, can be visited – when not working, of course – in the old canal company stables.

The **Leek** Branch, which makes such a dramatic diversion from the main line at Hazelhurst Junction, leaping across a bold stone aqueduct as the canal proper drops through the locks below, clings to wooded slopes almost all the way to Leek. About a mile before the town it crosses a large pool, popular with local anglers, before entering a 130 yd (120 m) tunnel. The branch ends on a splendid stone aqueduct over the Churnet. The final half mile of the waterway was filled in and used for industrial development some years ago.

The canal engineer James Brindley spent part of his life in Leek, working as a millwright. Brindley Mill, a working corn mill equipped by him, is open to the public and is in Macclesfield Road.

Addresses

Birmingham Canal

Brochures/reservations

Alvechurch Boat Centre Ltd,
Scarfield Wharf,
Alvechurch,
Birmingham B48 7SQ
Tel: 021 445 2909

Associated Cruises,
Victoria Basin,
Lock Street,
Wolverhampton
Tel: 0902 23673

Brummagem Boats Ltd,
Sherborne Street Wharf,
Birmingham B16 8DE
Tel: 021 455 6163/0691

Trent and Mersey Canal and Caldon Canal

General information

Heart of England Tourist Board,
2/4 Trinity Street,
Worcester WR1 2PW
Tel: 0905 613132

Brochures/reservations

Anglo Welsh Waterways Holidays (base at Great Haywood)
Canal Basin,
Leicester Road,
Market Harborough,
Leicestershire LE16 7BJ
Tel: 0858 66910

Black Prince Narrowboats (base at Stenson)
Stoke Prior,
Bromsgrove,
Worcestershire B60 4LA
Tel: 0527 575115

Canal Cruising Co. Ltd,
Crown Street,
Stone,
Staffs ST15 8QW
Tel: 0785 813892/812620

Jannel Cruisers Ltd,
Shobnall Marina,
Shobnall Road,
Burton-upon-Trent,
Staffs DE14 2AU
Tel: 0283 42718

Shardlow Marina Ltd,
London Road,
Shardlow,
Derbyshire DE7 2HJ
Tel: 0332 792832

Swan Line Cruisers Ltd,
Fradley Junction,
Alrewas,
Staffs DE13 7DN
Tel: 0283 790332

MIDLAND RINGS

Boats lock through from River Severn to Staffs and Worcs Canal at Stourport

One of the marvellous things about the English canal system is the way you can duck and weave from one waterway to another, completing circuits so that you don't have to retrace your steps, and in this chapter we look at three which offer a wide variety of cruising ground.

Four Counties Ring

A favourite circular route with seasoned boaters is the Four Counties Ring which covers the counties of Staffordshire, Shropshire and Cheshire and just touches on a corner of West Midlands. The canals that link them are the Staffordshire and Worcestershire, Shropshire Union, and the Trent and Mersey. There's a fair bit of boating to be done on the route – about 135 miles (216 km) and more than a hundred locks – so allow a good two weeks to complete it. There is plenty to see, too, along the way.

As with any circular route, of course, there is a choice of starting points, but we'll set off from Great Haywood, Staffordshire, which happens to be a favourite of ours. It is a charming place, every inch a canal village standing at the junction of two great waterways – the Staffs and Worcs, heading almost due south to Stourport, and the Trent and Mersey which strikes off in two directions, north west towards Preston Brook and on a looping westerly course towards Long Eaton, Nottinghamshire. For the sake of argument we'll begin with the southerly route.

Staffordshire and Worcestershire Canal

The work of canal genius James Brindley, the Staffs and Worcs was completed in 1772, linking the River Severn with the Potteries and the expanding industries of the Midlands. Despite ferocious competition from other canal companies, it managed to remain profitable until the mid-1800s when the railways really began to make their presence felt. Like many other waterways, it fell into decline this century, but was saved by the post-1960s leisure boom.

Great Haywood is one of those villages which owe their existence to a great, if eccentric, aristocratic clan, in this case the Ansons,

Lockside cottage on Staffs and Worcs Canal

family name of the Earls of Lichfield, whose seat is the nearby Shugborough Hall. The original village was within the area that is now Shugborough Park but the Ansons, their fortunes waxing, bought it up, knocked it down and moved the villagers into Great Haywood so that the family could enjoy peace, privacy and a view unspoilt by the sight of the lower classes at home. Another of their self-indulgences is an elegant ironwork bridge which crosses the Trent and Mersey just south of the junction. It was built so that the Ansons could travel to church, grandly, by horse and carriage. Until the bridge was built they had to trudge, dustily in summer, muddily in winter, the staggering distance of 300 yds (270 m)! Today the bridge is used by the hoi polloi, crossing between canal towpath and village. Nearby, a medieval packhorse bridge stirs the imagination as it crosses the River Trent.

Now owned by the National Trust, **Shugborough Hall** is open to the public and houses collections of French and English china, silver, paintings and furniture. The Staffordshire County Museum, located in outbuildings, re-creates scenes from nineteenth-century life, including original kitchens, laundry and brewhouse. Shugborough Park Farm is a working farm museum illustrating farm life in Georgian times. It has rare and historic breeds of livestock and a working flour mill. 'Noah's Park' is a special area in which children can make friends with domestic and rare breeds of animals and poultry.

A delightful towpath bridge marks the junction of the Trent and Mersey and the Staffs and Worcs, which starts in a very pleasing basin now used as a hire-boat base by Anglo Welsh Narrow Boats. The canal leaves the basin by a narrow exit which is, in fact, an aqueduct over the River Trent. Ahead lies a 21-mile (33.6 km) trip through some of the finest of England's countryside: from the grandeur of Cannock Chase, to woodlands, meadows and heathland. For the first mile or so you might think you are navigating on The Broads rather than a narrow-gauge canal. This area is known as the Tixall Wide, rich in kingfishers. The watercourse narrows again at Tixall Lock, the first of twelve between Great Haywood and Autherley Junction.

The canal continues along the Sow Valley, following the River Sow to the village of Weeping Cross where it picks up the River Penk. At Milford it crosses the Sow on a James Brindley aqueduct. Weeping Cross is the nearest point on the canal to the historic old town of Stafford, about 1½ miles (2.4 km) away. There is a regular bus service. The M6 motorway dogs the waterway for a couple of miles (3.2 km) between Acton Trussell and Penkridge, but canal scenery makes up for the noise. Penkridge, a large village, has good facilities for the boater – a selection of shops and pubs, and moorings above the lock.

Beyond Penkridge, the Staffs and Worcs jigs about a bit, flirting with the M6 again for a little while, then darting under the A5, the old Roman Watling Street, before going into more contortions. It straightens out again at Coven, a village with several shops and a launderette. A narrow cutting, reached just after Foster Bridge (No. 68), will not take two boats side by side, so someone needs to be up for'ard keeping an eye open. Autherley Junction, where we join the Shropshire Union on the next stage of our tour, lies on the right soon after the Blaydon Road bridge.

Shropshire Union Canal

Autherley Junction (not to be confused with Aldersley Junction, half a mile (0.8 km) to the south where the Staffs and Worcs is joined by the Birmingham Canal Navigations) has been a busy and important waterways location since 1830 when Thomas Telford connected the Birmingham and Liverpool Junction Canal with the Staffs and

Worcs. The Shroppie begins at a stop lock with a mind-reeling fall of 6 ins (15 cm) – it was intended to separate the waters of two rival companies, rather than serve the usual practical purpose. Ahead is a journey of 42 miles (67 km) and 29 locks to Barbridge, where the Middlewich Branch sets off to meet the Trent and Mersey. Most of the locks are in the second half of the journey – there are some 8 miles (13 km) to the next lock, at Wheaton Aston, followed by a 17-mile (27 km) lock-free stretch to the five Tyrley Locks just outside Market Drayton.

Some care is called for in navigating the Shroppie's early stages because there are three stretches on the way to the village of Brewood, 5 miles (8 km) from Autherley Junction, where the canal enters rocky cuttings too narrow for two boats to pass. An ornate balustraded stone bridge tells us that we are nearing Brewood. This is Avenue Bridge (No. 10 on the Shroppie), and it takes a private driveway across the canal to Chillington Hall, seat of the Gifford family for 800 years. The canal was cut through parkland designed by 'Capability' Brown, and the bridge was the canal company's sop to an anxious landowner. North of Brewood, where the elegant, cast-iron Stretton Aqueduct carries the waterway across the A5 trunk road, is Belvide reservoir where the Royal Society for the Protection of Birds has an extensive nature sanctuary.

North of Wheaton Aston, the Shroppie continues in an almost straight line with just a few curves following the contour line. To the east there are good views towards Cannock Chase. Bridge No. 26 at Church Eaton is a good example of a roving bridge, designed to allow horses towing boats to cross the canal without the towline being unhitched. Appropriately enough, this one is called Turnover Bridge. Just before the village of **Gnosall Heath** (treat the G as you would in the word 'gnat') comes Cowley Cutting where the canal is cut through some 700 yds (630 m) of solid sandstone, entering the 81 yd (73 m) Cowley Tunnel on the way. The whole cutting was originally intended to be a tunnel, but there were dangerous faults in much of the rock. Gnosall Heath is a useful stop with shops and the Boat Inn at Bridge No. 34 and the Cotton Mill canal shop, housed in an old steam-powered flour mill, and the Navigation Inn at Bridge No. 35.

Beyond Gnosall Heath the canal abandons cuttings in favour of embankments. To the west, on the other side of Telford New Town is The Wrekin, 1,335 ft (400 m) high. Then comes **Shelmore Embankment**, a mile-long monument to the back-breaking, heart-breaking work of canal construction in the days before mechanical diggers and dumpers. It took a gang of up to 600 men and 70 horses five and a half years to shift the millions of cubic feet of earth needed to build the embankment. Time and again the construction collapsed, and Thomas Telford, the gifted engineer in charge of the project, died before it was completed in 1835.

Shelmore Embankment leads to Norbury Junction – which it no longer is! Until 1944 a branch of the Shropshire Union led off from here to Shrewsbury by way of a long flight of locks. However, Norbury remains a busy canal settlement with a British Waterways maintenance yard. Bridge No. 39, known as High Bridge, is an unusual double-arched structure. The lower arch was added as a strengthening buttress. Beyond the bridge the canal enters the dense, jungle-like Grub Street Cutting. followed about a mile later by another embankment, the Shebdon, only half a mile (0.8 km) long this time, but an awesome achievement nonetheless. Today, trees screen the surrounding landscape, and the boater who thinks that's a shame might care to reflect on what navigation would be like on a windy day without the trees.

The Shroppie passes from Staffordshire into Shropshire between Bridges 47 and 48. At Goldstone Wharf, next to Bridge 55 is the Wharf Tavern, changed most certainly since 1939 when it was visited by L. T. C. Rolt, author of *Narrow Boat*, but still a popular waterside pub. Doubtless the navvies of old could have done with it when they dug out the next landmark. Woodseaves Cutting, more than a mile long, was hewn from solid rock, again without the aid of machinery. Care is needed when passing approaching boats. The cutting leads us back across the border into Staffordshire. A row of Tudor-style cottages, dating in fact from 1837, marks Tyrley Wharf. The cottages were built by the owner of the nearby Peatswood Hall. Saved from near-dereliction in recent years, they have now been converted into an attractive canal-ware shop.

Departure from Tyrley means it is time for the crew to start flexing their muscles again, for immediately ahead are the five Tyrley Locks, taking the canal 33 ft (10 m) down on the approach to **Market Drayton**, where we find ourselves in Shropshire once again. Market Drayton is a very pleasant canalside town where an open-air market is held every Wednesday as it has been for the past seven hundred years. This is the home town of the British Empire hero, Clive of India. There are two boatyards here and plenty to do, even if it isn't market day.

The locks come thick and fast between Adderley and Audlem: five at Adderley, taking the Shroppie down 31 ft (9 m), and fifteen at Audlem with a total fall of 93 ft (28 m). The locks at Adderley have been dubbed 'Adderley Park' because of their trim condition. The last of the locks at Audlem, a pleasant village with a butter market and fifteenth-century church, leads us on to the Cheshire Plain.

Nantwich is a compact market town: picture postcard attractive yet unselfconscious in its no-nonsense approach to life. For centuries it was Britain's main salt-mining centre. There are many fine half-timbered Tudor-style buildings. The Tollemache Almshouses, in London Road, were built in 1638 by Sir Edmund Wright, who went on to become Lord Mayor of London. The canal basin here is a waterways frontier: the original terminus of the old wide-gauge Chester Canal from Nantwich to Ellesmere Port, then junction with the Birmingham and Liverpool Junction Canal. The town centre is a twenty-minute walk from the basin. A small local museum, emphasising the town's role in the salt trade, is in Pillory Street.

North of Nantwich the Shroppie crosses lush pasture land and at Hurleston Junction, after about an hour's cruising, passes the start of the Llangollen Canal. Soon after the Barbridge Inn, on the right, the Middlewich Branch begins.

Middlewich Branch

It's downhill all the way from Barbridge Junction to Middlewich, an exciting 10-mile (16 km) journey with 4 locks and 31 bridges. The Middlewich Branch of the Shroppie is one of those delightful canals that instils a sense of adventure the moment your boat enters it. It passes through some really beautiful countryside, and in places is more like a young river, winding through lush meadows or on the edge of deciduous woodland. In others it alternates between wooded cuttings and high ground.

The waterway begins at Barbridge with a roving bridge, and for close on half a mile (0.8 km) you steer with care between a colourful collection of narrow boats and cruisers moored on either side. But the bustle of busy moorings is soon left behind. After soaring across the River Weaver on a high embankment and aqueduct the canal reaches the village of **Church Minshull**, a charming Cheshire village immortalised in that gem of canal literature, L. T. C. Rolt's *Narrow Boat*. Beyond the village we have little but herons, the occasional kingfisher, and cows for company, and the only reminder of the twentieth century comes when the London–Glasgow railway line crosses the canal, its 125 mph (200 kph) InterCity expresses a sharp contrast to the sedate speed of traffic on the water. The branch steals up on Middlewich, sliding past back gardens, under four bridges and into Wardle Lock where it drops, unexpectedly, it seems, into the Trent and Mersey Canal.

Trent and Mersey Canal

The section of the Trent and Mersey between Middlewich and Kidsgrove is covered in the chapter on the Cheshire Ring, so let's start this final run of the Four Counties Ring at the great **Harecastle Tunnel**. Three tunnels have been cut through Harecastle Hill since 1777 when the first one, built by James Brindley, was completed. An engineering sensation at the time, that first tunnel, 1¾ miles (2.8 km) long and with no towpath, soon became a bottleneck, for boats had to be 'legged' through – men lying on the boat's roof 'walked' it through with their feet on the roof of the tunnel. Thomas Telford came to the rescue with a second tunnel built alongside the first and opened in 1827. This one had a towpath, and it's the one still in use today. Until the beginning of this century both tunnels were used on a one-way basis, but the original tunnel was affected so much by subsidence from coal workings that it had to be abandoned. The third tunnel, built to carry the Stoke–Kidsgrove railway through the hill, was closed in the 1960s. Navigation through the 2,919 yd (2,627 m) tunnel now in use is controlled by a tunnel-keeper.

Harecastle Tunnel leads the Trent and Mersey into the heartland of the Potteries, and a flight of five locks takes it 50 ft (15 m) down through the centre of industrial **Stoke-on-Trent**, one of the 'Five Towns' (though in reality there were six) immortalised by the writer Arnold Bennett. The City Museum and Art Gallery, in Bethesda Street, Hanley, houses one of the most outstanding collections of ceramics in the world, including work from China, Greece, Rome and Egypt. Just above the Stoke Top Lock is the junction with the very pretty Caldon Canal.

South of Stoke, at Bridge 104, **Barlaston**, you can moor up and visit the Wedgwood Pottery visitor centre. It has a huge range of products on exhibition and it tells the story of the development of this well-known ware. There is a small charge for entrance. Below Meaford power station the countryside becomes a bit more undulating and less industrial. All boaters on this route should stop at the busy but friendly town of **Stone** to pay homage to the Wyatt family, of the Canal Cruising Company, who were pioneers in the field of narrow-boat holiday hire. Their yard is the group of mellow brick buildings with a dry dock near the winding hole between locks 29 and 28 in the Stone flight. No need to call on them personally – just drink their health with a pint of Bass in the delightfully mellow Star Inn right beside Stone Bottom Lock.

The canal continues westerly through the villages of Burston, Sandon and Weston, where it passes close to the site of the Battle of Hopton Heath, a major conflict in the Civil War. It took place on 19 March 1643, went on all day with Roundhead musketry answering Cavalier cannonfire – but in the end neither side could honestly say they had won. From Hoo Mill Lock the River Trent accompanies us to complete the Four Counties Ring back at Great Haywood.

Stourport and Avon Rings

Alvechurch Boat Centre, a progressive hire company with bases at Alvechurch, in rural Worcestershire, and at Gayton, Northampton-shire, sensibly suggests a number of circular routes to potential clients. The brochure is especially helpful and informative, indicating three different ways of getting from one base to the other, plus possible side trips, in addition to the 'Rings'. Moreover, it runs a useful 'short breaks' facility right through the season. (Short breaks are usually available only in early and late season.) This means you can have half a week afloat, starting on a Monday or Friday, and, better still, you can book two, three or four short breaks in a row at discounted prices. The company has a large fleet of narrow boats. Let's examine two of Alvechurch's suggested circular routes – the Stourport Ring and the Avon Ring.

The Stourport Ring has 116 locks in 86 miles (138 km) and cruising time is estimated at 48 hours – which, says the brochure, 'can usually be reduced to 40 hours with a crew of four or more'. Forty-eight hours doesn't sound too bad – averaging around seven hours a day over a week. But it doesn't allow for much sightseeing, pottering around pretty villages, socialising in canalside pubs, stop-ping for a morning's fishing, chatting to other boaters at locks, moor-ing up to keep the helmsman dry when it rains, mooring up to allow some uninterrupted sun bathing . . . Or for engine trouble (unlikely, but possible), or for stopping to help someone else with a problem. Make it a fortnight or take a series of consecutive breaks to give eleven nights. Today's waterways are used mainly for leisure and relaxation, not the beat-the-clock rush and dawn starts that the old carrying companies expected from their employees.

The Tontine Pub, a focal point for boaters in the Canal Basin, Stourport

The suggested anti-clockwise route from the Alvechurch base on the Worcester and Birmingham Canal takes you through to the Birmingham Canal Navigations and Gas Street Basin then on to the Staffordshire and Worcestershire to Stourport-on-Severn, a delightful inland port with a vast basin. Here you transfer to the River Severn and cruise to Worcester, returning to the Worcester and Birmingham for the home run back to the hire base.

The Avon Ring is Alvechurch Boat Centre's most popular two-week cruise. The brochure estimates 58 hours to cover the 108 miles (173 km) and 139 locks – 'It can be completed in one week provided you have an energetic crew and can make an early start each day.' And provided you're not delayed by rivers flooding. The route goes by way of the Tardebigge flight of 30 locks and Worcester, then on to the Severn to Tewkesbury and the junction with the River Avon. The Avon takes you to Evesham and on to **Stratford**, where there are moorings close to the Shakespeare Memorial Theatre. (Book in advance if you want to see a performance.) The southern section of the Stratford Canal gets you to Kingswood Junction, then the northern section links up with the Worcester and Birmingham Canal at Kings Norton Junction about two hours' cruising from Alvechurch.

Addresses

General information

Heart of England Tourist Board,
Trinity Street,
Worcester WR1 2PW
Tel: 0905 723394

North West Tourist Board,
The Last Drop Village,
Bromley Cross,
Bolton BL7 9PZ
Tel: 0204 591511

Staffordshire and Worcestershire Canal

Brochures/reservations

Bijou Line Holidays,
Ponkridge Wharf,
Penkridge,
Staffs ST19 5DX
Tel: 078571 2732

Double Pennant Boatyard Ltd (base at Autherley Junction)
Hordern Road,
Wolverhampton WV6 0HT
Tel: 0902 752771

Gailey Marine,
The Wharf,
Watling Street,
Gailey,
Staffs ST19 5PR
Tel: 0902 790612

Gregory's Canal Cruisers (base at Autherley Junction)
Oxleymoor Road,
Wolverhampton
Tel: 0902 783070

Teddesley Boat Company,
Park Gate Lock,
Teddesley Road,
Penkridge.
Staffs ST19 5RH
Tel: 078571 4692

Shropshire Union Canal

Brochures/reservations

Anderson Boats,
Wych House Lane,
Middlewich,
Cheshire CW10 9BQ
Tel: 060684 3668

British Waterways Leisure,
Nantwich Marina,
Chester Road,
Henhull,
Nantwich,
Cheshire CW5 8LB
Tel: 0270 65122

Countrywide Cruisers (Brewood) Ltd,
The Wharf,
Kiddiemore Green Road,
Brewood,
Staffs ST19 9BG
Tel: 0902 850166

Holidays Afloat Ltd,
The Boatyard,
Market Drayton,
Shropshire TF9 1HH
Tel: 0630 2641

Ladyline Ltd,
Bretton Road,
Market Drayton,
Shropshire TF9 1HH

Middlewich Narrowboats,
Canal Terrace,
Middlewich,
Cheshire CW10 9BD
Tel: 060684 2460

Trent and Mersey Canal

Brochures/reservations

Canal Cruising Co. Ltd,
Crown Street,
Stone,
Staffs ST15 8QW
Tel: 0785 813982/812620

Staffordshire Narrow Boats (base at Stone)
Equity House,
42 Central Square,
Wembley,
Middlesex HA9 7AT
Tel: 01-903 2081

Stourport and Avon Rings

Brochures/reservations

Alvechurch Boat Centre Ltd,
Scarfield Wharf,
Alvechurch,
Birmingham B48 7SQ
Tel: 021 445 2909

WATERLUDE: HIRE BOAT OPERATOR

James Hoseason

James Hoseason is director of Hoseasons Holidays Ltd, of Lowestoft, Suffolk, which his father founded in 1945. He has vigorously campaigned to improve the Broads environment, and that of canals and rivers in Britain, through various organisations and associations, including the Inland Waterways Amenity Advisory Council, on which he served for eight years.

'Because our waterways in Britain have little or no commercial traffic, there's no danger in boating on them. They are very safe and pleasurable to navigate. As a consequence both the indigenous Britons and overseas visitors can go boating without a navigator's certificate.

'We get a great many mainland Europeans boating in this country, notably the Germans, the Swiss and the Scandinavians. The majority of the Swiss – all those jokes about the Swiss Navy! – go to the wide beam waterways of the Broads, the Fens and the Thames. They do go on the canals, too. They have little opportunity of boating at home. They are very bossed about in their own country and they love going where there are not many controls.

'We as a company have boating in each of the UK waterways except in Ireland. We are involved in a big way in France and Holland.

'When you first get aboard the hire boat you listen to the operator and as soon as he's gone you try to go as fast as you can, because the motor car has ruined our temperament compared with our fathers' and our grandfathers'. But you find that the boat only goes a certain speed – a slow speed. When that speed becomes your speed, the therapy is biting – the enormous therapy and pleasure which comes from that slow, steady exploration of that other side of Britain.

'The French are just awakening to the pleasure that sits on their back doorstep, the waterways. It's worth studying the background there. The system was kept going after World War II in order to decrease the amount of transport on the roads. For example, the River Seine is fascinating. You sit there and watch a huge barge linked to another huge barge, followed by a tug at the back pushing five hundred motor cars from Paris to Le Havre, to be put on a ship to go to Los Angeles or perhaps to Boston Harbor. Those five hundred cars are not on the railway, they're not on the road. They put them on the river. It's a brilliant system.

'The only navigation that lends itself to commercial use in the UK is the Yorkshire navigation. British Waterways Board has made a heavy investment there to make it work. You can go coast to coast, into the Leeds–Liverpool Canal and out the other side into an area where pleasure boaters don't go, to the commercial side right down to the Humber.

'I have a tremendous affection for the Norfolk Broads. I've done a great deal of canal exploration up and down this country. I've boated in France, in Scotland, in the Fens and on the Thames, and I enjoy it all.

'Another thing about an inland boating holiday is that you share the waterway with the real residents – the wildlife. The ducks and swans are out early in the morning and they come and peck-peck-peck-peck on the side of the boat. You feed them, and you can see the wildlife in a setting that is totally natural, and get friendly with them. This is a great thrill.

'I was born a farmer's son near Southwold, Suffolk. My father came from the Shetlands. To survive there is a combination of being a seaman and a farmer. My father was harbourmaster at Lowestoft during World War II. After the war he set up on his own doing charter work, and we had about two hundred people a year taking boating holidays with us. I trained as a civil engineer, but I joined the business in 1950 when my father was ill. We have grown and grown. Fourteen million people have taken holidays with us – that's homes as well as boats because we do self-catering, too. These days we've got the largest boat-booking organisation in the world.

'I have three sons, all very keen on boating. When they were young we used to take two boating holidays a year. One of the pleasures of taking children on a boating holiday is the contrast with the motor car. In a car it's terrible for the children. They sit in the back. Dad drives endlessly and they really have no function apart from waiting for the next stop for a cup of tea or an ice cream.

'Put them on the cut and you keep on coming to a lock, and they're as important as you are, because there are the sharing bits. You send them ahead and they lower the paddles. You've got lifejackets on them and if they do fall in, as may happen, you fish them out.

'You have total freedom on a boating holiday. You can get up and go to bed when you like. You can have a cup of tea or a glass of whisky when you like. It's a freedom holiday. With so many other holiday services you're tied in to a chain of timetables. But go boating and you're free from what has been called the tyranny of service.

'I think the era for concern about the future of the Broads should now be over, because Lord Belstead said in the House of Lords when he introduced the Norfolk and Suffolk Broads Act that Britain's newest and most exciting national park was being created.

'People have been hiring boats on the Norfolk Broads since before World War I. We've got a copy of the earliest brochure – 1894.

A man called Brown was doing it. In those days you could rent a 50 ft [15 m] yacht with accommodation for six people, with two servants aboard – a skipper and a steward – for £6 a week.

'There was a very short season of twelve weeks at the most. The crew devised the brilliant idea of having birthdays. The steward would say: "You ought to know, guv'nor, it's Harry's birthday on Tuesday." There would be a couple of quid for that. The following week the skipper would touch his forelock and say: "I wonder if you know it's Bert's birthday on Friday, sir?"

'The motor cruiser was devised in the inter-war years, in the late twenties and early thirties, and of course it has progressed and progressed since then. Another progression was from 1960 upwards when the standard of living – and expectation, therefore, of cosseted comforts – grew and grew, and we put aboard hot and cold running water, self-starting engines, refrigerators, modern cookers and television.

'Business is on the move the whole time. We are adapting the whole time. There's a constant need to anticipate tomorrow's business.'

GRAND UNION CANAL

Narrow boat entering a lock at Stoke Bruerne

Providing a continuous link between the River Thames and Bir-mingham, with a final section connecting with the Trent in Leicester-shire, the splendidly named Grand Union Canal is the backbone of the entire English inland navigation system. Strictly speaking, it's a composite of at least eight canals, built at various times.

The concept of a Grand Junction Canal was a brilliant finishing touch to the age of waterway transportation, and like most great ideas it was mothered by necessity. Until its completion in 1800 boats from the Midlands had to follow the circuitous routes of the Fazeley, Coventry and Oxford Canals, trans-shipping their cargoes to lighters at Oxford for a further trip of about 100 miles (160 km) to London. The new route, from Braunston, Northamptonshire, to Brentford, Middlesex, cut the entire journey by 60 miles (96 km) and with its wider locks the Grand Junction could carry 70-ton (70.6 tonnes) barges. Other canals soon linked it to Warwick and Bir-mingham, Market Harborough and Leicester from where the River Soar provided a connection with the Trent. In 1820 the Regent's Canal was opened, providing a link between the Grand Junction at Paddington and the Thames at Limehouse. In 1929 the various waterways making up the system – some with narrow gauge locks – were consolidated into the Grand Union Canal Company. England's great waterway remained in commercial use until well into the 1950s – it did sterling service during World War II – but decline was inevitable. Fortunately, it remains intact – just over 160 miles (256 km) of boating pleasure, to say nothing of the network to which it provides access.

Regent's Canal

Many people might not expect much of a waterway that starts in the big ships' ambiance of Limehouse Basin and ends, 22 miles (35 km) and 12 locks later, among the factories and warehouses of suburban Hayes. Yet the Regent's Canal is an intriguing, even adventurous, run. Holiday boaters not using their own craft can put the idea of entering the Thames out of their minds. Hire companies are not at all keen on their boats being subjected to the perils of a busy tidal waterway. Some commercial traffic – especially timber barges – still uses Limehouse Basin and the lower reaches of the canal, so care is needed when navigating. The basin, once crowded with shipping of all sizes, is now being developed as a residential and office complex surrounding a marina.

The canal climbs out of Limehouse Basin in five locks that take it through Mile End and Globe Town, where the Hertford Union Canal leads 1½ miles (2.4 km) to the River Lee. Victoria Park, 300 acres (121 hectares) of open space, comes as a reminder that even in built-up London there is still some room to breathe. Hemmed in as it is for the most part by factories and the anonymous back walls of houses, the canal nevertheless enjoys a peculiar privacy, and it is hard to believe that the everyday life of places like Bethnal Green and Islington is going on all around as your boat slips quietly along. At Islington the canal goes into a 960 yd (864 m) tunnel.

Just after Camden Town, beyond the last lock for 27 miles (43 km), the canal reaches one of the best-known of London's 'lungs' and presents one of the best views of Regent's Park and London Zoo, whose aviary designed by Lord Snowdon is a striking landmark. Passing within a good throw of Lord's cricket ground, we reach one of the most elegant stretches of urban waterway in Britain – an area of neatly painted bridges and fine canalside properties – before sliding into the short Maida Hill Tunnel. A further short stretch of waterway leads to famous Little Venice with its colony of narrow boat residents. There are lots of interesting pubs and restaurants in the area, which is within easy reach of the West End's fleshpots.

The Paddington Arm of the Grand Union strikes off to the west through the paralysingly dismal suburbs of Kensal Green – a huge cemetery here, and a sighting of Wormwood Scrubs Prison to liven things up – Harlesden and Park Royal. Through Greenford, Norwood and Southall the canal snakes towards Bulls Bridge Junction where it joins the main line 6 miles (9.6 km) from its terminus at Brentford and 137 miles (219 km) from Salford Junction on the outskirts of Birmingham.

Grand Union Canal (Main Line)

Kew Gardens, Syon House – with its collection of paintings and fine period furniture, as well as its Capability Brown gardens – and the National Music Museum can all be visited with ease from Brentford, where the canal locks through to the Thames, which is tidal up to Teddington Locks. For its first 12 miles (19 km) or so, the main line climbs steadily through an area of gradually diminishing suburbia, reaching truly open space at Denham, north of Uxbridge. Watford, surprisingly, provides a lovely setting for the canal to pass through. Not the town itself, though – that is avoided in favour of the splendid Cassiobury Park, formerly owned by the Earls of Essex.

The Grand Union begins to climb more steeply as it draws nearer to the Chiltern Hills and 17 locks take it through Apsley, Hemel Hempstead, Boxmoor, and Bourne End to the agreeable Hertford-shire town of Berkhamsted, where a ruined castle looks down on the waterway from one side and an Indian totem pole from the other. William the Conqueror was offered the English crown in the castle in 1066. The totem pole is the trade mark of a local timber yard. Nearby is the headquarters of **Bridgewater Boats**, whose Castle Wharf base has won an environmental award. The company's fleet of narrow boats, each named after one of T. S. Eliot's 'practical cats', are very comfortably and sensibly fitted out. More yards need to realise that boats are for relaxing on, as well as sleeping in. It's not much fun crowding round an inadequate table, or lying on a plastic-mattressed bunk on wet days.

Eight more locks lift the canal out of Berkhamsted, through North-church and on to Cowroast, where the summit is reached. Downhill from the summit lock, on the opposite side of the rather busy main road, is the seventeenth-century Cow Roast Inn, large, clean, friendly and most welcome after all that uphill work. The British Waterways workshops at Bulbourne signal the end of the summit and the approach of two arms of the canal. The **Wendover Arm**, whose junction is at Bulbourne, is navigable to small craft for a short distance. Its chief use is as a feeder for the summit, although there are plans to restore it. Seven locks carry boats down 42 ft (13 m) to Marsworth Junction, where the Aylesbury Arm veers off to the west, getting off to a good start with a descending flight of eight locks.

The **Aylesbury Arm** is a very satisfying diversion. Only 6½ miles (10 km) in length, it nevertheless has 16 locks and takes the best part of a day to negotiate. But its rewards are many: superbly peaceful countryside, good pubs and a dramatic terminus in a large pictur-esque basin close to the centre of Aylesbury. A busy market town, Aylesbury is well worth a visit. It has a number of attractive squares, and some Georgian buildings. Buckinghamshire County Museum, in Church Street, illustrates local crafts and costume as well as archaeology and natural history.

The main line continues beyond Marsworth, passing a licensed canalside shop before descending towards the villages of Ivinghoe and Slapton. Carved into the chalk on Dunstable Downs, and visible from the canal, is the Whipsnade White Lion. Nearly 500 ft (150 m) long, he's been lording it over the countryside since 1935. At Grove

Two Bridgewater boats from Berkhamstead lock through at Marsworth

the River Ouzel moves in on the canal, accompanying it into the picturesque Bedfordshire town of **Leighton Buzzard**. This is the place where a choir boy has to stand on his head every 23 May while a seventeenth-century will is read out to the crowd. It is part of a custom which includes the beating of the parish bounds and arises from a bequest in which Edward Wilkes founded a row of almshouses in 1633.

At Fenny Stratford and Bletchley the Grand Union is back in Buckinghamshire, meandering with the Ouzel to the tiny village of Little Woolstone. A long, lockless stretch takes it across lightly wooded countryside to the brave new town of Milton Keynes with its shopping malls, Open University and concrete cows.

Twelve rural miles (19 km) beyond Milton Keynes take us to **Stoke Bruerne**, the archetypal canal village. Lovely old cottages, a pub and a couple of shops cluster round the Grand Union, and a former warehouse has been turned into the admirable Waterways Museum, in which the story of the waterways system, more than two hundred years old, is told. Among the many exhibits are items of clothing and cabin ware, engines, pieces of equipment, a reconstructed boat cabin – even a traditional narrow boat. Stoke Bruerne, justifiably, is a very popular place, and no doubt plays an important role in encouraging interest in the country's waterways.

As if Stoke Bruerne were not enough, the Grand Union then presents another canal spectacular: the country's longest navigable waterway tunnel. Blisworth Tunnel is 3,057 yds (2,751 m) long and has no tow path. Fortunately, though, it is wide enough to allow two 7 ft (2.1 m) narrow boats to pass each other. When the Grand Junction Canal was opened in 1800 cargoes were unloaded at each end of Blisworth Hill and sent on their way by tramway. This was because initial attempts at digging a tunnel had failed. However, human determination and ingenuity succeeded and in 1805 – on 25 March – the tunnel was inaugurated. As you motor through, spare a thought for the poor fellows who had to 'leg' boats through its length of about 1¾ miles (2.8 km). For the record, the country's longest canal tunnel is at Dudley, but this is navigable at present only to trip boats operating from the Black Country Museum.

West of the village of Blisworth is Gayton Junction where the Northampton Arm heads off to the north. The arm is 5 miles (8 km) long and has 17 locks, all fairly easy to work. **Northampton** has seen it all – from the trial of Thomas à Becket, to much military activity during the Civil War. For a time it was even the capital of England. Today it is a major centre for the manufacture of footwear. Best place to moor is below the bottom lock in the River Nene.

After Gayton Junction the main line continues for 12 miles (19 km) or so of big farm country to Norton Junction, where the Leicester Section peels off to the north to connect, eventually, with the River Trent. The main line continues by way of the village of Welton and the Braunston Tunnel, 2,042 yds (1885 m) long and passable for two 7 ft (2.1 m) beam boats. **Braunston** itself is an important canal centre, for here is the historic junction with the Oxford Canal and the start of that time-saving, money-saving, mile-upon-mile-saving waterway of 1800. For the next 5 miles (8 km) to Napton Junction the route was shared by the old Grand Junction and Oxford canal companies. At Napton the main line branches north towards Birmingham while the Oxford Canal strikes off to the south.

After close on 10 miles (16 km) of fairly empty arable land, the canal reaches the imposing town of **Royal Leamington Spa**. A spa town, it was mostly developed in Victorian times, but is none the less a place of considerable dignity. Leamington virtually merges with **Warwick** after the Grand Union has crossed the River Avon. Warwick Castle is a superb example of medieval fortification. It contains a collection of paintings which includes works by Rubens, Velazquez and Van Dyck.

About 7 miles (11 km) north-west of Warwick, the large village of **Kingswood** is reached. Here is the junction with the Stratford-on-

Avon Canal, marked by an iron turnover bridge split to allow a horse to pass from one side of the canal to the other without being unhitched from the tow rope. Beyond Kingswood the main line continues for about 14 miles (22 km) to Bordesley Junction, deep in the heart of Birmingham, where it gains access to that great underrated network of waterways, the Birmingham Canal Navigations.

Addresses

General information

Heart of England Tourist Board,
2/4 Trinity Street,
Worcester WR1 2PW
Tel: 0905 613132

London Tourist Board,
26 Grosvenor Gardens,
Victoria,
London SW1W 0DU
Tel: 01-730 3488

Thames and Chilterns Tourist Board,
The Mount House,
Church Green,
Witney,
Oxon OX8 6DZ
Tel: 0993 778800

Brochures/reservations

Blisworth Tunnel Boats Ltd,
The Wharf,
Gayton Road,
Blisworth,
Northants NN7 3BN
Tel: 0604 858868

Braunston Boats Ltd,
Bottom Lock,
Braunston,
Northants
Tel: 0788 891079

Bridgewater Boats,
Castle Wharf,
Berkhamsted,
Herts
Tel: 044 27 3615

Calcutt Boats Ltd,
The Locks,
Stockton,
Rugby CV23 8HX
Tel: 092 681 3757

Concoform Marine,
The Boatyard,
High Street,
Weedon,
Northants NN7 4QD
Tel: 0327 40739

Cowroast Marina Ltd,
Cowroast,
Tring,
Hertfordshire
Tel: 044 282 3222

Grebe Canal Cruises,
Pitstone Wharf,
Leighton Buzzard,
Beds LU7 9AD
Tel: 0296 661920

High Line Yachting Ltd,
Mansion Lane,
Iver,
Bucks SL0 9RG
Tel: 0753 651496

Kate Boats Warwick,
The Boatyard,
Nelson Lane,
Warwick CV34 5JB
Tel: 0926 492968

Sovereign Narrowboats (base near Leighton Buzzard)
Pinkertons,
Atbara Road,
Church Crookham,
Hants GU13 0JZ
Tel: 0252 615103

Warwickshire Fly Boat Co.,
Shop Lock Cottage,
Stockton,
Rugby CV23 8LD
Tel: 092 681 2093

Waterways Holidays,
Union Canal Carriers Ltd,
Canalside,
Little Braunston,
Daventry,
Northants MM11 7HJ
Tel: 0788 890784

Weltonfield Narrowboats,
Weltonfield Farm,
Welton,
Daventry,
Northants NN11 5LG
Tel: 0327 842282

Whilton Marina Ltd,
Whilton Locks,
Daventry,
Northants NN11 5NH
Tel: 0327 842577/849335

Wyvern Shipping Co. Ltd,
Bossington Wharf,
Rothschild Road,
Linslade,
Leighton Buzzard,
Beds LU7 7TF
Tel: 0525 372355

THE SOUTH

Sign at Newbury, Berkshire

While the Midlands and North of England offer many and varied cruising grounds, the South hasn't missed out on the canal and river scene. The Thames and a sizeable chunk of the Grand Union with its several arms have been responsible for introducing many of the vast South Eastern population to the pleasures of inland boating, or at least gongoozling. Many of them have been encouraged to sample the waters elsewhere. The Oxford Canal is ideal for novices, and the almost fully restored Kennet and Avon will be attracting ever-increasing numbers.

There's no such thing as a North/South divide in waterway cruising. The system is almost totally interconnected, and there's a steady two-way flow of traffic.

The Thames

Much has been written in prose and poetry in praise of the Thames. Deservedly. To cruise between its navigable beginnings at Lechlade and its tidal reaches past the Palace of Westminster is to take a liquid route through history. It is also to marvel at the wealth in this part of Britain – and to dig deeper in your pocket for a meal or snack ashore than you would almost anywhere else in the country.

The non-tidal Thames offers some 124 miles (198 km) of navigation between Teddington and Lechlade, and here we explore some of the highlights as far as Oxford, which is the turning point for many hire boats. The entire non-tidal length of the river has more than forty locks.

The Thames is wide and beautiful, and abundant in 'Private – No Mooring' signs. It can be irritatingly packed with boats on warm weekends in summer when everyone gets afloat at the same time – tacking sailing dinghies, canoes, inflatables, motor launches, modest cruisers, hire craft and gin palaces, and everyone has a right to be there. It's OK while you're on the move, but queueing at the locks and trying to find a peaceful place to moor on the towpath side can be a problem at times. On weekdays, even in high summer, the pressure is eased, and this is the time to visit some of the attractive Thameside towns and villages.

Purple loosestrife, rose bay willow herb, brooklime, yellow flag, ladies' smock and blue skullcap are among the plants that bloom on the river bank or at the water's edge. From June to August you'll see yellow water lilies floating on the surface. Mallards, mute swans with flotillas of cygnets, coots and moorhens, diving crested grebes, pochard and teal share space on the water, while herons, wagtails, reed buntings, sandmartins, reed warblers, swallows, swifts and martins and the occasional kingfisher seek their food in its environs. Anglers, out in force in the coarse fishing season (mid-June to mid-March), may fill their keepnets with dace, chub, roach, tench, perch, carp and barbel.

While most people are enjoying the surface activities and interests which the Thames provides, there's one sector whose favourite habitat is underwater. A number of diving clubs use the river. Keep an eye open for their marked boats. Obliging divers are sometimes extremely helpful to boating people, retrieving items that have been accidentally knocked overboard.

Negotiating Thames locks downstream of Oxford is painless. Each has its own lock keeper, and the opening hours are displayed at each lock. Boats queue for a place, and the lock keeper packs them in, presses the buttons and sends them on their way, beckons in the group of craft from the opposite direction and repeats the exercise. All you do is switch off the engine and send a crew member ashore to adjust the ropes.

If it's peace you want on the Thames, you can usually find it, but impromptu parties can take place – and why not? – and if you're moored cheek by jowl with other craft, you could find yourself listening to someone else's reggae or rock far into the night when you'd been hoping for nightingales. Or maybe you're having a knees-up on board and irate, pyjamaed neighbours thump on your cabin windows at one o'clock in the morning, asking you if you know what time it is. It's a matter of give and take, and the more crowded the river, the less give and take there's likely to be. The strictly ungregarious should time their Thames holiday for spring or early autumn. The river is lovely at all seasons.

Narrow boats are indigenous to the canals, but river cruisers come into their own on the Thames, and there are some magnificent specimens to be seen. About 15,000 powered craft are based on the river, some of which seem to be pure status symbols which never leave their moorings. Many, however, from 'jelly moulds' to lovingly restored Thames launches, from purpose-built cruisers to converted lifeboats, are the pride and joy of their owners and regularly make weekend or extended voyages.

Hiring boats

Between them, hire companies on the Thames offer a selection of more than five hundred boats. The Thames Hire Cruiser Association ensures that its members' craft are of a high standard, and a special benefit to hirers is that they can moor overnight at boatyards belonging to members. Hotel boats provide a really relaxing way to see the Thames, and several companies offer a good service. One of the most distinctive is the two-deck *Le Sans Egal*, which cruises between Eton and Oxford and also offers special event packages for Ascot Races, Henley Regatta and the Henley Festival of Music and Arts. It accommodates eight guests in roomy cabins with private facilities. Another luxury hotel boat, the *Actief*, has half- or full-week cruises on the Upper Thames and the 70 ft (21 m) *Tranquil Rose*, in narrow-boat style but 12 ft 6 ins (3.75 m) wide, sleeps nine in six cabins, some with en suite toilet. *Tranquil Rose* cruises between Maidenhead and Oxford, sometimes adding Windsor to the itinerary, providing competitively priced seven-day holidays and first-class food.

The wide, majestic Thames is renowned for its scenery, but some reaches are truly magnificent. Part of it is in an area designated as of outstanding natural beauty.

People with boats registered on the canal system can enter the Thames at Oxford, having equipped themselves in advance with a Thames licence.

Shopping for supplies should present no problem on the river. Well-kept towns, easily accessible from the water, are found along its length.

To cruise the non-tidal Thames, allow at least a fortnight. It's a pity to rush, with so much sightseeing along the route. Because there is such variety, we are giving a fairly detailed guide to attractions ashore. One of the first, above Teddington Lock, is **Hampton Court Palace**. Mooring overnight at nearby Hampton Wick wharf is free. You may see the replica paddle steamer *Lucy Fisher*, a trip boat which operates from Runnymede. Thames Ditton, Sunbury and Weybridge are on pretty stretches of water. Between Staines and Chertsey is the huge Penton Hook Marina, produced out of redundant gravel pits.

At **Runnymede**, a temple commemorates the signing of the Magna Carta in 1215, and nearby is the memorial to President John Kennedy on an acre of American territory – the land was donated to the USA by Britain. Both are at **Coopers Hill**, about a mile from Old Windsor Lock. At the top of Coopers Hill, from where the view is splendid, is the Commonwealth Air Forces Memorial, in a formal garden. It commemorates the 20,000 airmen who died in World War II. Admission is free.

Windsor Castle, dating back to the time of William the Conqueror, dominates the waterside scene and occupies about 13 acres (5 hectares). It costs nothing to wander in the precincts, which are nearly a mile around. There's an admission charge to see the State Apartments (closed to the public when the Queen is staying there), Queen Mary's doll's house, designed by Sir Edwin Lutyens, the Queen's presents, the royal carriages, the exhibition of drawings and St George's Chapel.

Another place to visit in Windsor is the Royalty and Empire Exhibition at the Central Station. It recaptures Queen Victoria's Diamond Jubilee in 1897, with Madame Tussaud's wax figures at the event and the Royal Train standing at the platform. Seventy Coldstream Guards are on parade and a hi-tech presentation depicts events during Victoria's long reign.

An iron bridge crosses the Thames to Eton. The famous college is open to the public in the afternoons. Casting off again, **Monkey Island** is the next landmark. It is privately owned but there are moorings for boat people going to the restaurant. Through the lock is peaceful Bray, once the living of the famous vicar immortalised in song. He changed his religion five times between the reigns of Henry VIII and Elizabeth I.

An elegant eighteenth-century road bridge and a brick railway bridge dated 1838, the work of Isambard Kingdom Brunel, span the river on the approach to Maidenhead and Boulter's Lock. Boulter's is alive with colourful crowds passing the time watching queues of boats go through.

As you cruise towards Marlow between the beechwoods of the Chilterns the scenery gets better and better. The **Cliveden** reach is spectacular. The gardens at Cliveden, Taplow, former home of the Astor family, sweep down to the water's edge, and are open daily to the public between March and December. Parts of the house, which stands high above the Thames, can be visited on Thursday and Sunday afternoons between April and October. Cliveden hit the headlines in the 1960s during the Profumo Affair as the setting for frolics which cost a cabinet minister his job. Anyone interested in stately homes should allow for a leisurely visit. There's a lot to see – 400 acres (160 hectares) of gardens, woods, pavilions, sculptures, temples and the amphitheatre where *Rule Britannia* was first performed in 1739. Cliveden, now owned by the National Trust, is leased to a hotel group.

Cookham is where the painter Stanley Spencer was born, and where he painted local scenes populated with his distinctive bulbous figures. A permanent exhibition of his work is on show in the village, and his painting *The Last Supper* is in the twelfth-century parish church. Sir Stanley died in 1959.

Cookham is one of the places where the annual swan-upping ceremony takes place – a sort of cygnet census. In July the Royal Swan Keeper – for decades a member of the Turk family – investigates every cygnet of the many swan families between Sunbury and Pangbourne, to check its identity. If its parents have certain marks on their beaks, showing they are owned by the Dyers Company or the Vintners Company, the cygnet is given a similar mark. Cygnets of swans with unmarked beaks are likewise left unmarked – they belong to the Queen.

Marlow has an impressive suspension bridge and some good waterside restaurants. The famous Compleat Angler Hotel is on one side, and All Saints parish church on the other. Marlow's literary connections include T. S. Eliot, Percy Bysshe Shelley and his wife, Mary.

After Medmenham Abbey, for a time the base of RAF Signals Command, is Hambledon Lock – a place to set the cameras clicking, with a picturesque mill and wide weir. Photographers will also find inspiration at **Henley**, where the Royal Regatta is held in the first week of July. Thankfully the town is no longer a bull and bear baiting centre, though some of its old coaching inns where the 'entertainment' took place remain. More than three hundred buildings are listed as of special architectural or historic interest.

Beyond Henley, Shiplake and Wargrave are on opposite banks of the Thames. The poet Tennyson, who had been courting a lawyer's daughter for fourteen years, married her at Shiplake in 1850. Jerome K. Jerome, author of *Three Men in a Boat* was often a customer at Wargrave's George and Dragon Inn. These stretches, right up to Goring, are in an area designated as of outstanding natural beauty. Sonning, with a waterside churchyard and one of the most glorious lockside gardens on a river where every lockside is well maintained and decorative, attracts crowds of gongoozlers.

Now we come to Reading, where the lively can seek out the nightspots. The River Kennet joins the Thames near Caversham Lock, and Blakes Lock, a short cruise from the confluence, gives access to the Kennet and Avon Canal. This has been the subject of a great restoration drive to re-open the route from the Thames to the Bristol Channel. Reading Borough Council has provided riverside walks, one of which is designed to feature the Forbury Gardens by the remains of Reading Abbey. The walks are marked with a reflected swan logo.

One of the oldest watermills on the Thames is at **Mapledurham**. It dates back to the fifteenth century and opens to the public at weekends between Easter and September. Wheat is ground, using wooden machinery and millstones. A trip boat takes passengers from Caversham Bridge to Mapledurham House and the watermill. Nearby is Westbury Farm Vineyard, where conducted tours (and tastings) are available. Here, too, are trout-stocked lakes where a day ticket could lead to a fresh-caught fish supper for the crew.

On to **Pangbourne**, with its iron tollbridge and wide, wide weir, and the reaches where Kenneth Grahame set *Wind in the Willows*. Grahame spent his last years in Pangbourne, at Church Cottage. He died in 1932. The tollbridge leads over the water to Whitchurch and its beechwoods.

Historic house addicts will want to see the classical Georgian **Basildon House** and its 400-acre (160 hectares) park, open in the afternoons from Wednesday to Sunday between April and October. Right beside the river is the Child Beale Wildlife Trust, with birds, animals, statues and riverside walks. It opens daily from mid-March to December.

Goring and Streatley are well-kept villages either side of the river, linked by a bridge which provides a superb view. The lovingly restored Magdalen College barge is an uplifting sight. During several lock-free miles to Wallingford, we come to the Beetle and Wedge at Moulsford, featured as The Potwell Inn by H. G. Wells in *The History of Mr Polly*.

Wallingford has a 17-arch, 900 ft (270 m) bridge carrying road traffic over the Thames. A grassed area by the water gets packed on warm summer days. Beyond Benson, near Day's Lock, and actually on the River Thame, which flows into the Thames here, is the Roman town of **Dorchester**, where Thomas Hardy set *The Mayor of Caster-bridge*. It has some attractive sixteenth- and seventeenth-century buildings. Close to the town are the important sites of Maumbury Rings, a Stone Age or early Bronze Age amphitheatre, and the pre-historic earthworks of Maiden Castle. Dorchester Abbey contains a museum which opens daily in summer except on Mondays. One of the biggest antique showrooms in England – Halliday's Antiques – is in Dorchester, in a fine Georgian building. Craftsmen making fire surrounds and mantelpieces in eighteenth-century French and English style can be seen at work.

Clifton Hampden's brick bridge is an impressive structure of the 1860s. On the eastern bank is the Barley Mow, the thatched inn which was a favourite with Jerome K. Jerome. He stayed there while writing his famous book. Another pub can be reached by going through Clifton Lock and hairpinning left into the original channel. Go as far as it's navigable and you're there, at The Plough at **Long Wittenham**. In the village is the Pendon Museum, which has railway relics dating from the early nineteenth century on display, as well as rural scenes from the 1930s. It is open on Saturday and Sunday afternoons.

Another place to stretch your legs is **Sutton Courtnay**. Moor near Culham Lock to admire the village and its churchyard, whose occupants include Lord Asquith, prime minister from 1908 to 1916, and Eric Blair, alias George Orwell.

Now we come to **Abingdon**, a busy market town with a long expanse of moorings. Overlooking the river is the former Napoleonic prison which became a grain store and is now an arts and leisure centre, with swimming pool and bar. Abingdon, in Oxfordshire since the 1974 boundary changes, used to be the county town of Berkshire, and the County Hall houses a museum. In Thames Street are the remains of buildings of the medieval abbey.

Near Sandford Lock and the 'Sandford Lasher', as the mighty weir is known, is the Radley College boathouse, below Nuneham Park, a mansion built in 1756 with later Capability Brown touches. It is a conference centre and not open to the public.

Five miles to Iffley Lock and now we're in **Oxford**. Iffley's twelfth-century St Mary's Church is famous for its Norman features. Below Folly Bridge are the college boathouses and Christ Church Meadow where the River Cherwell joins the Thames. By the bridge, which is known as Head of the River, is an inn of the same name, converted from a grain warehouse.

To see any of the city's wealth of architecture you'll have to go ashore because the river doesn't provide much of a view. You may be gone some time. In the square-mile core of the city alone there are at least six hundred listed buildings. Oxford has one of the world's greatest libraries, the Bodleian, established in 1602 and containing five million books. It has the Ashmolean, Britain's oldest museum, founded in 1683, pre-dating the British Museum by sixty years. It has a Museum of Marmalade, too, in the original High Street premises where Frank Cooper started selling his wife's conserve in 1874.

Most of the colleges' quadrangles and chapels are open to the public in the afternoons. Christ Church, one of the largest colleges, was founded in 1546, and Worcester College, in Beaumont Street, is noted for its gardens.

Little Clarendon Street has an assortment of specialist shops, and the covered market between Market Street and High Street has a lot of interesting stalls and shops. Oxford Craft Centre is based here, with works of local artists on sale. Dealers offer an incredible range of wares at the Antiques Centre housed in an old jam factory opposite the railway station in Park End Street. In St Aldates is Alice's Shop. Alice, of *Wonderland* fame, a daughter of the Dean of Christ Church, bought her sweets here as a child in the 1860s.

As well as half a dozen museums, Oxford now has a hi-tech show, *The Oxford Story*, in which you can take in the sights and sounds of the city and its university covering eight centuries with the aid of the latest audio-visual techniques.

Oxford is as far as we're going on the Thames, though the river is navigable through a dozen more locks to Lechlade through increasingly peaceful, pastoral countryside.

Oxford Canal

Let's take the Oxford in one gulp (metaphorically), which means including the part which isn't strictly south, geographically. The canal goes between Hawkesbury Junction, near Coventry – the site of two IWA Festivals in recent years – and Oxford. Its length is nearly 80 miles (128 km), it has 43 locks, numerous lift bridges, and to cruise it your boat has to be under 7 ft (2.1 m) wide. Its southern sections have become very popular, so for the quiet life avoid the high season. In early and late summer the Oxford is pure bliss for those seeking rural isolation. There's just one high decibel zone: if you're not turned on by the exciting intrusions of low-flying jets, wear ear plugs to go through Upper Heyford, where there's a US Air Force base, and Lower Heyford.

Be prepared for some self-catering. There are pubs and restaurants on the route, and the odd village, but they're not too thick on the ground. Others are within walking distance, sometimes a mile or two away, usually along narrow lanes where the grass grows high on the verges. Be sure to walk on the right to meet oncoming traffic, and to squeeze into the side when a combine harvester comes along. Remember, setting off eagerly for a meal is one thing. Walking back in the dark and looking for the spot where you moored your boat is another.

Be prepared, too, for a succession of lift bridges. Benevolent local farmers leave most of them raised, but you may have to provide the muscle power now and again. Make sure no-one is on the roof or they could have unpleasant contact with the underside of the bridge.

At Oxford access to or from the Thames is via a railway swing bridge and the narrow Isis Lock, or by Duke's Cut, 3 miles (5 km) above Oxford, which avoids the city. You can transfer from the Oxford Canal to the Grand Union at Napton Junction or Braunston, and into the Coventry Canal at the northern limit at Hawkesbury Junction.

The River Cherwell and the canal run close together for miles. At Thrupp there's a row of well-kept cottages standing parallel to the navigation, and thanks to the thirsty working boatmen of the past two centuries, this small community and the visitors to its waterway are served by two canalside pubs, the Boat and the Jolly Boatman.

Somerton Deep Lock drops the canal 12 ft (3.6 m). Abandoned at the helm of a small boat while the crew busies itself high above, one feels the devil incarnate may materialise at any moment.

Banbury in the early 1960s was a blot on the waterscape – a place to get through as quickly as possible. It has improved since then, but not much. Romantic childhood notions of seeing a fine lady upon a white horse at Banbury Cross (a nineteenth-century copy of the original version which the Puritans destroyed in 1602) seem at odds with the dismal scene from the water. The bakehouse where spicy Banbury cakes were made fell to the demolition squad in 1964, but they are still available, packed with currants, and one shop provides customers with an updated recipe. A nice touch, that.

The canal basin at Banbury was filled in long ago to provide a site for the bus station. Steam on to **Cropredy**, scene of the 1644 battle when the Royalists beat the Roundheads and saved Oxford. Refreshments and gifts can be bought at Cropredy Wharf, and there are two good pubs handy for the canal, the Brasenose Inn and the Red Lion.

Halfway through the five locks to Claydon summit is bridge 145, leading to **Claydon** village, which has a post office and stores, a church and a pub – and the Granary Museum (admission free) where a nineteenth-century kitchen is reproduced. Agricultural implements and mechanism, and relics galore, are displayed, and there's a gift shop.

The long, narrow, straight stretch of water at **Fenny Compton** is where there used to be a tunnel. It was taken down in the late 1860s, but seems to haunt the canal to this day. There's a strange stillness, the greenery grows claustrophobically high at either side and the mosquitoes and horse flies are downright vicious.

Following a lock-free course that twists and turns, ducking under low brick bridges, we reach Napton Top Lock and Marston Doles, a little place which developed with the canals and declined when the railways came. We are now in Warwickshire. Steer round a bend or two, and there's a vista of **Napton Hill**, with its windmill proudly restored, and the downhill sweep of the Napton Locks. This is a magic place. For one thing, there's a farm shop *with an off licence* at Holt Farm, near Green's Lock. (It closes at 7.30 pm.)

For another, a walk into Napton village reveals an amazing collection of mechanical instruments which includes a Wurlitzer, a barrel organ, a Compton cinema organ and a mechanical violin. You have to book in advance for the occasional concert (Tel: 092 681 2183).

North of Napton is the junction with the Grand Union Canal, and 5 miles (8 km) further on is Braunston Junction, where there's a big marina. The Grand Union branches off towards Birmingham and the Oxford goes steadfastly on for miles without let or hindrance, village or lock, only the odd bridge, to Hillmorton. Once through these three narrow locks you're skirting Rugby. Within a short stretch there's an aqueduct over the Avon and a 250 yd (225 m) tunnel built when the bends were ironed out of the Northern Oxford in the 1820s. This is Newbold Tunnel, with a towpath either side. Newbold Wharf has two old inns next door to one another, the Boat and the Barley Mow.

With the railway for company, and the M6, you reach Hawkesbury Junction. The Oxford Canal comes to a halt, and Coventry is just around the corner.

Kennet and Avon Canal

This is a canal with many points of interest and variations of scenery. It has a few swing bridges, the first of which is the worst, travelling westward, requiring strong arms. It is at Theale, between Reading and Aldermaston, and the obvious thing to remember is to close the road traffic barriers, follow the displayed instructions and open the traffic barriers afterwards. It isn't a specially busy road so you shouldn't cause much delay to vehicles.

Since several long sections of this broad canal have been restored and re-opened to navigation, a healthy ecological balance has been noted. In the Melksham area, 190 plant species have been identified in a 4-mile (6.4 km) stretch of the canal. A wide range of birds and butterflies grace the waterway.

The few remaining gaps in the navigation should soon disappear, and restoration of the entire 75-mile (120 km) route between Reading and Bath – beyond which the tidal section starts to Bristol Docks,

Avonmouth and the Severn Estuary – should soon be complete. Between Reading and Avonmouth, a distance of just over 100 miles (160 km), there are 105 locks and, good news for many, about fifty pubs between Reading and Bath beside or near the water. Twenty nine of the wide locks are in a 2-mile (3.2 km) stretch at Devizes, most of them in an impressive straight flight at Caen Hill. Depending on whether you are travelling east or west, you have a glorious cruise of 15 lock-free miles either ahead of you or behind you to compensate for your efforts.

The Kennet and Avon Canal Trust has a canal shop and information centre at Devizes Wharf, and another at Newbury Wharf, with canal artefacts displayed. It also operates trip boats at several points along the canal.

Two rivers, the Kennet and Avon, were canalised to form a link between the Thames and the Severn at Bristol, and a navigation was dug between Newbury and Bath to complete the waterway. By the time waterways nationalisation came about soon after World War II, most of the Kennet and Avon had fallen into disrepair – and fifteen years later pressure groups were campaigning for its restoration. Their persistence paid off. The work was done by volunteers, British Waterways and young people on the Job Creation Scheme. Assuming that the waterway is fully navigable by the time you read this, we'll start from the Thames end.

A Thames licence applies for the first lock, Blake's, but from here onwards a British Waterways one is needed until the tidal section administered by the Port of Bristol Authority.

Care is needed after passing through Blake's Lock because the narrow River Kennet often has quite a flow on it and the weirs have a bit of a 'pull'. There are sharp bends along the urban section, and a traffic-light control – a rare sight on English waters – is provided. Once out of Reading, the waterway is mainly rural to **Newbury**. There are good moorings by Newbury Lock. Newbury Bridge is a magnificent balustraded structure in stone, dating back to the 1770s. Centuries-old weavers' cottages are reminders that the cloth trade pitched Newbury into prosperity. The Borough Museum reflects this. Take a look at the butterfly and moth section, too.

Some beautiful wooded country accompanies the course of the canal, alternating with open pastoral views. Then comes **Hungerford**, which has a lovely old high street and an antiques arcade. Early-season visitors to Hungerford should be prepared for a curious event celebrated on the second Tuesday after Easter. This is the medieval Hocktide Ceremony. To quote the Thames and Chilterns Tourist Board: 'You will see the ancient Court Leet meeting to elect

Lift bridge on the Kennet and Avon Canal, near Aldermaston

officers. Two Tutti-men and the Orange Scrambler visit every house in the High Street with commoners' rights, demanding a penny from the men and a kiss from the women.' The Orange Scrambler distributes oranges to the 99 commoners, all of whom then have a nail hammered in their shoes.

Westward through the Bedwyns, Little and Great, a single chimney comes into view. This marks the Crofton Pumping Station, built in 1809 and beloved of canal buffs. It pumps water to the summit level of the canal, and can be seen steaming on certain weekends in summer.

The towpath, an almost continuous public right of way by the canal, is interrupted at Bruce Tunnel, 502 yds (452 m) long. Chains along the walls can be used to haul along unpowered craft.

Pewsey town centre is half a mile (0.8 km) from Pewsey Wharf. Next comes **Devizes**, where what is claimed to be the world's longest and most arduous canoe race is held every Easter, the 125-mile (200 km) course having 77 locks. The Devizes–Westminster race began in 1948 with two contenders – Pewsey and Devizes. Since 1950 the event has been annual. More groups clamoured to take part, and now the event attracts teams, including the Army and the Navy, from many parts of Britain and Europe.

Near the lock at **Seend Cleeve** is a pub called The Barge. Call in to find out about the Wiltshire Giant, 8 ft 4 ins (2.5 m) in his socks, who once lived there – and to sample the local brew, Wadworth's. On to **Semington**, where the observant may detect the bricked-up side bridge which used to be the turning into the long-abandoned Wiltshire and Berkshire Canal, opened in 1810. It took a 50-mile (80 km) winding route to Abingdon.

Soon, about half a mile (0.8 km) from the canal course, the River Avon flows more or less parallel with and below the canal, both leading into **Bradford on Avon** but retaining their individuality. Set amid steep woodlands, Bradford on Avon is a lovely town with some fine architecture from the nineteenth century back into the distant past. The walk down from the canal wharf provides a good view of much of it. The river bridge has nine arches, two of which date back to the fourteenth century, and there is a domed chapel in the middle of the bridge. It served as a small prison in the seventeenth and eighteenth centuries. At Bradford Wharf there are some original buildings from the canal's heyday, a fourteenth-century tithe barn and a pub, the Canal Tavern.

Canal engineer John Rennie built the Kennet and Avon's splendid Dundas Aqueduct of Bath stone. It is best viewed from below, a short walk from the water. It is even more impressive than Rennie's other aqueduct at Avoncliff, closer to Bradford on Avon.

The Kennet and Avon and the railway have an on–off–on relationship during the journey to Bristol. As Bath is approached the two are close companions, and the Avon moves nearer to make up a threesome. Diesel trains spasmodically disturb the tranquillity, but only briefly. The Dundas Aqueduct carries the canal across the railway and the Avon Valley.

A mile and a half (2.4 km) west of the Dundas Aqueduct is another point of interest to industrial archaeologists, the unique **Claverton Pumping Station**, restored by the Kennet and Avon Canal Trust, assisted by Bath University engineering students. Designed by Rennie to pump water 47 ft (14 m) from the Avon into the 9-mile (14 km) canal pound between Bradford on Avon and Bath, using two 15 ft (4.5 m) diameter waterwheels, the 'Claverton Ram' still comes into action on occasional pumping weekends, giving the usual electric pumps a break. It is the only waterwheel pump of its kind on the canals of Britain. It was installed in 1813 and finally gave up the ghost in 1952.

Entering **Bath** by canal is the stuff of which memories are made. The vantage point from a hillside cut provides a beautiful view of much of the spa city. Past the Sydney Gardens, through a little tunnel beneath Cleveland House, once the headquarters of the

Kennet and Avon Canal Company, under two cast-iron bridges, the thrills continue. Remains of Roman bath buildings, the pump room, the Abbey founded in 1499, the elegant architecture, all await exploration. There are overnight moorings at the foot of Widcombe Locks – and now you're on the River Avon. Get the guide book and go and see the sights.

The only manned locks are at Hanham, in the tidal water approaching Bristol. Confident, experienced boaters for whom time is no problem may plan a cruise into the Bristol Channel and up the Severn. Most people no doubt regard Bath as the turning point, and prepare to see the Kennet and Avon from a different perspective.

River Wey and Godalming Navigation

At one time a family called Stevens owned the River Wey and Godalming Navigation. They were boat-builders and carriers working on the Surrey waterway for around a hundred years. In 1964 Mr Harry Stevens gave it to the National Trust, whose licences to cruise are issued at Guildford and Weybridge. National Trust members who produce their card can get a 10 per cent reduction on 7- or 21-day licences. The navigation of 19½ miles (31 km) between Godalming Wharf and Weybridge has 16 locks. It is partly a natural watercourse and partly cuts made by man, who recognised the value of straightening it out a bit. All but the 4-mile (6.4 km) Guildford to Godalming section was opened in 1653, the final section being added more than a century later. A narrow-boat hire company at Guildford, Guildford Boat House, also runs trip boats and a restaurant boat, the *Alfred Leroy*, which seats up to 49 guests. The 69-seat trip boat *Harry Stevens* gives cruises towards Godalming and through rural scenery to the mouth of the derelict Wey and Arun Canal. This was built early in the nineteenth century to link the Thames with the English Channel – and one day it may carry leisure boaters through some of the loveliest and most isolated parts of south-east England as volunteers tackle the enormous task of restoring it. Incidentally, in January 1989, 45 Wey and Arun Canal Trust voluntary 'navvies' shared the excitement of uncovering an old lock chamber on private land near Loxwood, West Sussex. After being unused for well over a century, it was found to be in reasonably good condition. It was built in 1813 and is one of 23 locks on the canal.

Handy moorings on the Wey and Godalming Navigation, near Woking

Already well on the way to complete re-opening after tremendous recovery work is another waterway which leads off the Wey and Godalming Navigation, the Basingstoke Canal.

Good half-week deals are available on the Wey and Godalming – at present the most southerly point of the inland waterway system – and weekend hiring is available all the year round. It is a wide waterway, the locks taking boats up to 13 ft 10 ins (4.2 m) beam. Those with a week's holiday usually go to the Thames via Weybridge. The two rivers contrast strongly. The Wey is relaxed, rural and uncongested, and the Thames in this region is alive with pleasure craft. School outings and educational cruises for field study groups can be booked. These cruises go between Guildford Boat House and Catteshall Lock 4 miles (6.4 km) away and take about two hours. Teachers' notes and questionnaires for children can be supplied when a reservation is made.

Although much of the Wey navigation is through tranquil country-side, there is easy access to the shopping facilities of such towns as Guildford, New Haw and Weybridge and the marina facilities at Pyrford, where there is a waterside pub, The Anchor – one of the most popular of several along the navigation.

Guildford is an attractive and interesting city, with its ped-estrianised main street on a sharp incline. The museum, housed in a building which is partly seventeenth-century, is next to the castle grounds. The noted Yvonne Arnaud Theatre, a memorial to the Guildford-born actress, is right by the water.

Basingstoke Canal

The Basingstoke Canal, built to carry timber to London and coal back to Hampshire, celebrates its bicentenary in 1996. 'Celebrates' is the word, because for many years this beautiful, wide, wooded waterway was a 30-mile (48 km) stretch of dereliction and decay between Basingstoke and Byfloot, Surrey.

In the mid-1960s the Surrey and Hampshire Canal Society was formed to save the canal. The first task was to bring the waterway into public ownership, which involved complicated legal issues, but eventually, in 1976, it became the property of Surrey and Hampshire County Councils.

Then began years of physical hard work in mud and filth by heroic volunteers, young unemployed people and skilled men working under the Manpower Services Commission. To add to the problem, the roof of the 1,230 yd (1,135 m) Greywell Tunnel at Odiham had collapsed in 1932. At the time of writing more than 21 miles (34 km) of the Basingstoke Canal, between Odiham and Pirbright, were navigable, and the prospect of opening the route to its link with the Wey and Godalming Navigation looked reasonably rosy, except that more complications had set in. Conservationists and cruising people had differing opinions about the canal's future.

The general state of the unrestored Basingstoke Canal was not repugnant to all. Various flora and fauna found it an ideal habitat. Bats colonised the Greywell Tunnel, and the Nature Conservancy Council called for restrictions on motor boating. This upset the boating fraternity. After all, the canal would never have existed if it had not been for boats. They argued that a canal doesn't have to be derelict to provide an environment for a wide variety of creatures and plants. As for the bats, they would be asleep in the daytime when boats were on the move. In any case, boats which went through the tunnel wouldn't get far beyond it, because the section between it and Basingstoke was sold off and closed years ago, the terminal disappearing under concrete and being replaced by a bus station.

Talks are continuing between the opposing factions, and it is devoutly to be hoped that the issue is soon amicably settled. Meanwhile, boaters enjoy using the canal, and two enthusiasts with faith and foresight have opened a boatyard with a hire fleet, Galleon Marine, at Colt Hill, Odiham. At present their clients can explore the usable navigation in half a week. Once the Woodham flight of locks re-opens, they will have access to the Wey, the Thames and most of the inland waterway system of the UK.

A craft that has introduced thousands of people to the navigable reaches of the Basingstoke in the past few years is the *John Pinkerton*, a 67 ft (20 m) trip boat owned by the Surrey and Hampshire Canal Society, and operated by members mainly in the Odiham and Aldershot areas. It can take more than fifty passengers, and its profits go towards restoration work.

River Medway

The River Medway's upper reaches pass through glorious Kentish scenery, with farms, hop gardens and oast houses. May is a good time for a cruise, when the orchards are in blossom. The river's drawback is that its navigable course is only 43 miles (69 km) long, and most of its waters are tidal. The non-tidal section – the only part open to boat hirers – is the 18 miles (29 km) between Tonbridge and Allington Lock.

However, plenty of boat owners use the river. There are marinas or boatyards at Yalding and Allington and they are always busy. The Medway is a great place for trail boats, which can be slipped at Yalding and Allington. People interested in castles, ancient buildings, medieval bridges, pretty villages and pleasant pubs will find plenty to keep them happy for a few tranquil days without venturing into the tidal section.

Castles overlook the river at either end of the non-tidal section. Tonbridge's Norman castle is open all year. Allington's thirteenth-century castle has a moat and a noted art and furniture collection. It opens to the public from 2.00 to 4.00 pm daily. It is owned by the Carmelite Order and is used as a Christian centre.

Maidstone, 2 miles (3.2 km) before Allington going upstream, is a useful shopping centre. The riverside area is pleasantly landscaped and the Archbishop's Palace and Kent's largest church, All Saints, dominate the bank.

Rivers Lee and Stort

So that we don't get involved with the big commercial boats, we'll consider these rivers between Enfield and the northern limits of the navigations – the Lee as far as Hertford and the Stort as far as Bishops Stortford. The Inland Waterways Association chose the Lee Valley Leisure Park at Waltham Abbey as the site for its 1989 National Waterways Festival. Developed in the 1960s, it was Britain's first regional park. It covers 10,000 acres (4047 hectares) and provides a range of water activities and other leisure pursuits.

The canalised Lee has long, straight stretches with 21 locks in its total length of nearly 28 miles (45 km). The Stort branches off it near Hoddesdon and is a more winding and more rural river – and shallower – than the Lee, which is a renowned fishing river. Anglers from Harlow and the London area flock there at weekends.

Over the years the Lee can be said to have had a hand in Britain's defences. The former factory where the Bren gun and the Lee Enfield rifle were made is near Enfield Lock, and gunpowder was manufactured at Waltham Abbey and transported on the Lee throughout the Napoleonic wars. King Harold, it is believed, was buried at Waltham Abbey after the Battle of Hastings.

Navigation on both rivers developed from the mid-eighteenth century with the demand for barley from arable Hertfordshire for the breweries of the capital. Malt barges sailed between London and riverside towns like Hoddesdon and Ware. Old maltings can be seen at various places, including Ware – also known for its waterside mills – Stanstead Lock and Sawbridgeworth.

Addresses

The Thames

General information

Thames Water Authority,
Vastern Road,
Reading,
Berkshire RG1 8DB
Tel: 0734 593333

Thames Hire Cruiser Assn,
19 Acre End Street,
Eynsham,
Oxford OX8 1PE
Tel: 0865 880107

Brochures/reservations

Abercrombie & Kent (*Actief*),
Sloane Square House,
Holbein Place,
London SW1W 8NS
Tel: 01-730 7795

Abingdon Boat Centre,
The Bridge,
Abingdon,
Oxon OX14 3HX
Tel: 0235 21125

Hobbs & Sons,
Station Road,
Henley on Thames,
Oxon RG9 1AZ
Tel: 0491 572035

Maidboats,
Ferry Yacht Station,
Ferry Road,
Thames Ditton,
Surrey KT7 0YB
Tel: 01-398 0271

Salter Brothers,
Folly Bridge,
Oxford OX1 4LA
Tel: 0865 243421

Thames Valley Cruising Hotel (*Tranquil Rose*),
Unit 2, Rugby Wharf,
Consul Road,
Rugby,
Warwickshire CV21 1NR
Tel: 0788 69153

R.J. Turk & Sons,
Thames Side,
Kingston Upon Thames,
Surrey KT1 1PX
Tel: 01-546 2434

UK Waterway Holidays,
Welton Hythe,
Daventry,
Northants NN11 5LG
Tel: 0327 843754

Oxford Canal

General information

Heart of England Tourist Board,
2/4 Trinity Street,
Worcester WR1 2PW
Tel: 0905 613132

Thames & Chilterns Tourist Board,
The Mount House,
Church Green,
Witney,
Oxon OX8 6DZ
Tel: 0993 778800

Brochures/reservations

Anglo-Welsh Waterway Holidays (Aynho base),
Canal Basin,
Market Harborough,
Leics LE16 7BJ
Tel: 0858 66910

Black Prince Holidays (Lower Heyford and Napton bases),
Stoke Prior,
Bromsgrove,
Worcs B60 4LA
Tel: 0527 575115

Kennet and Avon Canal

General information

Kennet and Avon Canal Trust,
Canal Centre,
Couch Lane,
Devizes,
Wiltshire SN10 1EB
Tel: 0380 71279

Brochures/reservations

Anglo-Welsh Holidays (base at Dundas)
Canal Basin,
Market Harborough,
Leicestershire LE16 7BJ
Tel: 0858 66910

Wessex Narrowboats,
Hilperton Wharf,
Hammond Way,
Trowbridge,
Wiltshire BA14 8RS
Tel: 02214 69847

Wey and Godalming Navigation

General information

National Trust,
Dapdune Lea,
Wharf Road,
Guildford,
Surrey GU1 4RR
Tel: 0483 61389

Brochures/reservations

Guildford Boat House,
Millbrook,
Guildford,
Surrey GU1 3XJ
Tel: 0483 36186

Basingstoke Canal

General information

Hampshire County Council,
County Hall,
Winchester,
Hants
Tel: 0962 841841

Surrey County Council,
County Hall,
Guildford,
Surrey
Tel: 0483 518800

Brochures/reservations

Galleon Marine,
Colt Hill,
Odiham,
Hants RG25 1AL
Tel: 025 671 3691

River Medway

General information

Medway Ports Authority,
High Street,
Rochester,
Kent ME 1PZ
Tel: 0795 580003

Brochures/reservations

Tovil Bridge Boatyard,
Beaconsfield Road,
Tovil,
Maidstone,
Kent
Tel: 0622 686341

Rivers Lee and Stort

General information

British Waterways,
Melbury House,
Melbury Terrace,
London NW1
Tel: 01-725 8000

Brochures/reservations

Boat Enquiries,
41–43 Botley Road,
Oxford OX2 0PT
Tel: 0865 727288

WATERLUDE:
THE BOATERS

Mark and Avril Grimes

Mark Grimes, a self-employed builder in Sussex, has been a regular narrow boat hirer for more than twelve years. When he married in 1987 he persuaded his bride, Avril, to risk a boating honeymoon. She knew little of canals and wanted to go to Tuscany. Inevitably, they had their first row on board, but the waterways worked their charm on Avril, and she is as smitten with them as her husband. Their ambition is to own a narrow boat and to live and work in a canal environment.

Mark was born in Burnley, Lancashire, in the 1950s, close by the Leeds and Liverpool Canal. 'I didn't realise what it was – just mucky water at the end of the garden, as far as I was concerned,' he says. Scarcely surprising since his family moved southwards when he was four years old.

Years later, he went into the building trade, working with a carpenter who was a dedicated canal man.

'He'd been boating for years, in the days when you had to walk miles to get a bottle of milk,' says Mark. 'He was always going on about the canals, so four of us at work decided to have a go. We hired a boat for a week. We went up the North Oxford, on to the Coventry and up the Ashby Canal. From the first day that was me hooked. You could go anywhere – Oxford, London, Birmingham, Stratford . . . I enjoyed it because I have a great interest in history. Being a builder, I was so impressed by how these people built the canals with pick and shovel, and here's me, nearly 250 years later, still using the waterways.

'You can moor where you like, within reason. There are few restrictions. If you want to go to a disco every night you can. If you want to be in the countryside all the time, you can do that.'

His fear is that as more people use the canals – many of them the 'wrong' people who want the trimmings of civilisation provided along the banks – more restrictions will be introduced. 'The canals can do without people who want to turn the country into the town,' he says.

The honeymoon trip, Avril's introduction to canal life, was between Napton and Fradley Junction, in a Calcutt hire boat. The first (and last?) row resulted from an unfortunate incident when Mark was resting below decks and Avril, alone at the tiller, found the 12-ton (12.1 tonne) all-steel narrow boat on a collision course with a nearby glass-fibre cruiser. Avril yelled, abandoned her post and fled down the steps to rouse Mark, who was not pleased.

Meanwhile, the cruiser's helmswoman gave a worthy demonstration of how to avoid trouble fast, and an elderly bystander on the towpath, who had seen it all before many times, laughed helplessly behind a gnarled hand. Mark, leaping off the bunk, arms flailing in panic, knocked the window fitment and ended up with a pair of curtains dangling round his ears. This set Avril into paroxysms of mirth. Mark couldn't see the funny side and stumped off alone, as soon as the chance arose, to seek solace in a pub.

'We'd only been married a week. You didn't give me a choice,' Avril accuses in retrospect. 'I'd wanted to go to Tuscany.'

'Yes, dear,' replies Mark. 'I soon talked you out of that. It was probably unfair of me, but since your initiation you've become a pretty good boating woman.'

Patronising words, but conciliatory.

Mark and Avril always take a fortnight's canal holiday. A week isn't enough for them. They have looked at a lot of hire craft and take every opportunity to cast an eye over privately owned narrow boats. As a result, they know exactly what they want when they get a boat of their own.

'It's got to be full length, even though some parts of the system won't be available to us,' says Avril. 'It's got to have a proper kitchen, with a hob. And I'm not going without my automatic washer and tumble drier. It must have plenty of working surfaces. It's got to have a proper bath – not a shower – though a half-size one will do. I want a lounge with log fire with a copper hood and free-standing furniture, including a sofa and plenty of bookcases. We want a double bed that stays made up – not one that drops down as a table in the daytime. We want fitted carpets throughout and somewhere in the bedroom to keep our clothes. We don't want much extra sleeping accommodation – a couple of bunks, perhaps so there should be enough space for what we want. We want plenty of room in the bow, with double doors leading from the saloon. We don't need a lot of space at the stern. And we'd have to have a house as well, for security reasons when we're old.'

Slightly exasperated, Mark casts his eyes heavenwards. After twenty years in the building trade, and as a qualified bricklayer, his ambition is to divert to something else, making a living on the canals. He has an original idea which fills a gap in the present tourism scene, and which seems so workable and viable that it would be unfair to outline it here, in case someone else recognises it as a nice little earner and gets in first. Furthermore, Avril goes along with it.

With his carpentry and electrical skills, Mark is keen to fit out a narrow boat himself, buying a good steel shell with tanks and fitted engine.

He has experienced a number of waterways, and is keen to show off his favourites to Avril. He likes the Trent and Mersey, the Staffs and Worcestershire, the Birmingham-Fazeley and the Birmingham Canal Navigations – an interesting one this, he says, recalling the hard work negotiating countless locks, including the flight of thirteen at Farmers Bridge to avoid being 'trapped' overnight amid six-storey buildings.

'Once you've got up to Gas Street Basin it's nice. From Worcester Bar in the Middle of Gas Street Basin you can cruise for an hour and you're right out in the country. You turn into the Stratford Canal and it's completely rural. In Stratford you can moor in the basin in the centre of the town, among all the monuments. Tourists are paying a lot for accommodation around there. Going by boat must be easily the cheapest way to see Stratford.

'I'm not surprised that the BCN isn't used more. You have to be streetwise as to what's going on and where you're going. But I was surprised how clean the water is. There were little fishes in the locks.'

Even for a lover of the country like Mark, the southern Oxford is a bit too far from civilisation. He and Avril prefer eating out to cooking on board, and opportunities to do so are few and far between.

Mark sees the waterways as a great leveller. 'Everyone has to do the locks. Do you know, they have a notice at the Foxton flight explaining how to work them? There was this Yuppie there, studying it. He was obviously a man of high intelligence and no logic. He had to read it several times to find out what to do. And 250 years ago, people with no education just took a look at a lock and worked out how to operate it.'

As Mark and Avril work to achieve their ambition and qualify to join the Narrow Boat Owners' Club, Mark reflects: 'I just want to live on a boat. I just want to be there on the canal, without any pressures, to go to a place on the canal and stay long enough to get to know the area and the people, then to move on to another place, doing a bit of work when necessary. That will be the fulfilment of my life.'

EASTERN ENGLAND

Traditional hire yachts at Wroxham Boatyard, Norfolk Broads

The Broads

To visit the busy little centre of Wroxham on the Norfolk Broads in mid-season can be faintly alarming if you're about to take a holiday afloat. Cruisers, day boats and the occasional sailing vessel are skimming along, just missing one another, shooting the low bridge, carrying out U-turns and generally resembling an aquatic version of a big city rush hour. Don't be fooled. This is only the bit that shows from the road. Once on board you can find quiet, isolated areas where you can listen to the bird song and the whispering of the reeds. You have almost 1,750 acres (708 hectares) of river and broad to explore, and it's not difficult to avoid the crowds.

Sailing boats

Although motor boats dominate the Broads scene, today, with a growing consciousness of green issues, there's an increasing tendency to go for sail. The number of sailing boats for hire is gradually expanding. In 1987, the latest year for which figures were available, there were fewer than 100 hire sailing boats (they have auxiliary motors) and 1,600 hire cruisers. The privately owned boats greatly outnumber the hire boats – nearly 2,000 cruisers and just over 1,000 sailing boats in 1987.

One company claiming to have 'brought back the yacht to Wroxham' is Barnes Brinkcraft, who bought up a fleet of thirty boats which were just vegetating. Some were traditional Sun Prince and Sun Dream wooden-built craft, fitted out in larch on oak or mahogany on oak, from thirty years old to fifty-plus. Built for the Broads, they have quite a following because they sail so well, explains Jill Thwaites, who runs the company with her husband, Brian, and their sons, Daniel and Matthew.

'It helps if people have been even dinghy sailing, but it isn't essential. Novices soon learn. Tuition can be given. One of our sons has trained with the Olympic Youth Squad, and we all sail as a family,' says Jill. 'Once you've seen the Broads by sailing boat, you don't want a cruiser any more. We're very pleased with the demand. The boats are easy to handle. People who haven't sailed before are thrilled to find how competent they are by the end of the week. They're converts for ever.'

Plans were afoot to take a moulding so that this highly regarded type of sailing boat could be reproduced in easy-to-maintain g.r.p.

Plenty of headroom on traditional hire yachts, Norfolk Broads

There are nature reserves all over the Broads. Barton Broad, accessible only by boat, is a nature reserve, and there's another, the Berney Marshes on the River Yare at **Berney Arms**. Here, Norfolk's tallest windmill (70 ft (21 m) and seven storeys high) is an Ancient Monument, built in 1870 and still going strong.

Various water sports are held at **Oulton Broad**, near Lowestoft, with its 130 acres (53 hectares) of navigable water, where several boatyards and Hoseasons' headquarters are located.

For more remote cruising, try the River Ant, a narrow tributary of the River Bure, and visit **How Hill** Nature Reserve, near Ludham, where Toad Hole Cottage is an attraction. This brick-built thatched cottage was the home of an eel-catcher. Now, restored and furnished as it would have been around 1840, it is the Marshman's Museum. On the way to Toad Hole Cottage there are three old wind pumps. At the cottage you can buy tickets for the Wildlife Water Trail, a worthwhile trip because the guide points out flora and fauna which you might never have noticed. You abandon your own boat and go quietly among the reeds aboard the Edwardian-style *Electric Eel* perhaps spotting rare dragonflies, swallowtail butterflies, marsh flowers and plants, cormorants and a range of waterfowl. The boat leaves How Hill Staithe every hour, and the 50-minute trip includes a short walk to a bird hide.

By now you may have become fascinated by birds, if you weren't before, taking pleasure in observing secret lives from a hide. There's one at **Cockshoot Broad**, a small expanse of 8 acres (3 hectares) near Horning. It is closed to navigation but you can moor at Cockshoot Dyke and follow the board walk through the marshes to the hide.

Cockshoot is an example of a 'dead' broad being restored to the healthy state it enjoyed a hundred years ago. Owned by the Norfolk Naturalists' Trust, it had had phosphorus-rich sewage effluent and nitrogen-rich agricultural slurry poured into it for years, resulting in shallow, cloudy water covering several feet of mud. Plant life, and with it the animal and bird life, dwindled.

With the co-operation of the Trust and many other organisations, and the practical help of a team of scientists from the University of East Anglia and people on the Youth Opportunities Programme, the Broads Authority spearheaded the revival of Cockshoot Broad. The Authority has its own conservation volunteers, known as the Beavers, who introduced 10,000 plants from the marshes, including water lilies, to the broad, and now at least a dozen species are thriving. The Cockshoot success story may lead to the restoration of other broads.

Hickling Broad, off the River Thurne, has a nature reserve where the shallow water attracts many different bird species, including migrant ospreys, spoonbills and avocets. It also has a wide range of wild flowers. There are walking trails and a water trail which offers the opportunity to survey the scene from a 60 ft (18 m) observation platform. Hickling is a great 500-acre (200 hectare) broad.

Don't miss **Ranworth Broad** on the Bure. It is closed to boats because it is a bird sanctuary, but there are moorings on adjacent Malthouse Broad, where there is a Broads Information Centre and a grocery store. You can walk through the Ranworth Marshes to the Norfolk Naturalists' Trust's Broadlands Conservation Centre, a thatched wooden structure floating on pontoons.

About a quarter of a million people a year cruise the Broads, most of them in wide-beamed, forward-drive boats which, frankly, are not too easy on the eye. The latest hulls are designed to limit bank erosion, and there's an element of the soap dish about some of them. But they are practical with smart interiors, plenty of space and they're very stable on the water.

You can see why some people go back to the Broads year after year. In the daytime they can find a retreat and commune with nature or read a book. In the evening they can socialise with their fellow holidaymakers and the locals in one of the many village pubs which are handy for the water. They can visit towns and villages by boat and explore such places as Wroxham and Potter Heigham, with their medieval bridges, Horning, Brundell, Reedham, Somerleyton, St Olaves, Beccles, Coltishall and many others. Eat a sandwich by the water and you will quickly be surrounded by ducks, geese, swans, starlings, sparrows and a chaffinch or two, all shamelessly cadging a few crumbs.

Altogether there are some three dozen broads, linked by the Rivers Waveney, Bure and Yare and their tributaries, the Chet, Ant and Thurne. The broads are known to have been originated by man when great depths of peat were cut for fuel.

Today nearly 130 miles (208 km) of broad and river are navigable. Speed limits vary from 3 to 10 mph (5–16 kph). Broads Authority inspectors equipped with radio transmitters patrol the waterways in marked launches, enforcing byelaws and helping in emergencies.

River Nene

However you pronounce it – Nenn at the Northampton end, Neen by the time you get to Oundle and beyond – the River Nene sorts out the men from the boys. The locks have guillotine gates which take a lot of winding to lift and drop, and there are 37 of them in the 60 miles (96 km) between Northampton and Peterborough. Correction – the one at Ditchford is a radial which takes even more winding.

However, the river doesn't get overcrowded, it flows languidly most of the time and it has many devotees who return year after year.

Wide-beam boats which are resident on the river or which come in from the Great Ouse and Middle Level Navigations, use the river. Those coming off the Grand Union Canal through the Northampton Arm have to be under 7 ft (2.1 m) wide. To get crews fit for what is to follow, the Arm has 17 locks in 5 miles (8 km), but they are narrow, easy ones, descending through pleasant countryside until industrial Northampton is approached at the bottom. The Nene has a Washland Flood Relief Scheme, which involved the provision of a new channel nearly 2 miles (3.2 km) long, on which no mooring is permitted.

Along much of the Nene valley there are gravel workings, some long since water-filled and used for dinghy sailing and other sports. The river's beauty ripens in the middle reaches, where villages with rich brown ironstone cottages are easily accessible. The first bridge

Taking it easy on Salhouse Broad

of note is at **Irthlingborough**. It is a fourteenth-century structure with ten arches. Roughly midway between Irthlingborough Lock and Lower Ringstead Lock, on the east bank, is the site of a deserted medieval settlement, Mallows Cotton Village.

Denford's thirteenth-century church is right beside the water, and the village store and sixteenth-century pub, the Cock, are a brief walk away. North of Thrapston is Titchmarsh, where the poet Dryden grew up. He was born at nearby Aldwincle in 1631. Wadenhoe is an attractive village, pleasantly wooded by the river, and the King's Head pub is handy. A mile or so away, above Lilford Lock, is Lilford Wildlife Park, with a lot of attractions, and just beyond the next lock, Upper Barnwell, old gravel workings have been landscaped and developed into a country park, with picnic sites.

Passing **Oundle** Marina, the river makes a wide curve around the stone-built town. Many of the lovely eighteenth-century buildings are occupied by Oundle School.

The smart estate village of **Ashton**, with thatched stone cottages built by the Rothschild family at the beginning of this century, is owned by nature lover, conservationist and author Dr Miriam Rothschild. The village inn is called the Chequered Skipper after a rare butterfly. Ashton has put itself on the international map as the home of the World Conker Championship. Contenders gather there on the second Sunday in October, and have done for many years, and the winner demonstrates his skill before the TV cameras.

A strong sense of history prevails at **Fotheringhay**. The fifteenth-century church stands above the river in open, pastoral scenery. Close your eyes and imagine a great castle dating back 800 years. Now little more than a grassy mound, it is the castle where Mary Queen of Scots was imprisoned and beheaded.

At **Wansford** the river is crossed by a twelve-arch bridge beside which stands the seventeenth-century coaching inn, the Haycock. There is a local tale of someone floating away on a haycock when the farmland in the valley of the Nene was flooded. A 5-mile (8 km) stretch of private railway track goes from Wansford to Orton Mere. Trips are operated by the Nene Valley Railway, whose steam loco-motives delight railway buffs. The locos come from several countries – France, Belgium, Germany, Italy, Denmark, Sweden and Norway – as well as Britain.

The approach to **Peterborough** is through the 500-acre (202-hectare) Ferry Meadows Country Park, which has a bird reserve, nature trails, walks, fishing, riding, camping, a garden centre and a lake for sailing. In the city there are moorings at the Embankment, close to the Cathedral and a big supermarket. A former grain barge at the Embankment has been converted into a floating Chinese restaurant.

Peterborough is usually the turning point for hire boats, though some crews take the long, poker-straight man-made cut to Dog in a Doublet Lock, after which the Nene takes its tidal course to the Wash.

River Great Ouse

Most locks on the River Great Ouse have guillotine gates like those on the Nene, but many more boats use the Great Ouse and there's a much better chance of sharing the lock work with other boat crews. Also like the Nene, the Great Ouse, navigable from Bedford, is tidal from a sluice lock – the Denver Sluice, which is the entrance to the Middle Level Navigation in the Fens. Denver Sluice is about 16 miles (26 km) from The Wash, compared with the 26 miles (42 km) between Dog in a Doublet and the sea.

The Rivers Cam, Little Ouse and Wissey, navigable to Cambridge, Brandon and Stoke Ferry respectively, join the Great Ouse on its journey north. The New Bedford 'River' takes a lockless 21-mile (34 km) straight course from Earith to Denver Sluice. It is tidal and hire boats are not permitted on this man-made short cut – which is no great hardship because using it would mean missing Ely. There are 17 locks on the 75-mile (120 km) long Great Ouse. The sixteenth is Hermitage Lock, just beyond Earith, going downstream, which leaves a stretch of about 10 miles (16 km) of exposed, flat, lock-free landscape to Ely.

It is a pleasant river to cruise, particularly between Bedford and Ely, where the scenery is interesting and often lovely, and there are some villages and little towns of character – St Neots, Godmanchester, Huntingdon, St Ives, Hemingford Grey. Bedford itself makes the most of its river. There is a fine Embankment, with good central moorings and well-kept public gardens. The stone bridge was completed in 1813. Trip boats operate between Bedford and Castle Mill Lock, some 2 miles (3.2 km) away. Castle Mill, Willington and Great Barford Locks have all been re-opened in recent years, and it is hoped that the navigation will eventually be extended above Bedford.

Bedford's most famous son is John Bunyan – actually, he was born at nearby Elstow. He wrote much of *The Pilgrim's Progress* during a long spell in Bedford Gaol. He was there between 1660 and 1672 for preaching without a licence. The Bunyan Museum in Mill street, Bedford, contains his chair, walking stick and tankard. The church at Elstow, on the A6 just outside the town, has stained-glass windows with scenes from Bunyan's works.

After leaving Bedford, the first lock encountered is at **Cardington**, a name to evoke memories for many who served in the Royal Air Force. A walk to the village is worth while. In St Mary's Church is a memorial to the victims of the 1930 R101 airship disaster.

Great Barford's riverside is a popular spot. There is a bridge with 17 arches. Moorings are close to the Anchor, a pub with a restaurant. All Saints' Church is also by the river. **Tempsford** is worth a stop, especially if you have children on board. The pub, another Anchor, provides them with an adventure playground and a playroom, and on Sunday evenings in summer there are puppet shows. There are lovely, winding stretches of water at **Eaton Socon**, where anglers and picnic parties, as well as boaters, congregate. Services at River Mill Boats include engine repairs and bottled gas exchange. Books and maps are on sale, and there is a bar, restaurant, tea room and garden centre.

St Neots Marina is by the bridge. There are berths for visiting boats. A tall paper mill stands just outside the town by St Neots Lock, which is embarrassingly close to a road – people like to stand around watching you wind the deep guillotine gate. Those who keep counting reckon it takes five hundred turns to lift or lower the gate.

The peace of Offord Lock, between the villages of Offord Cluny and Offord D'Arcy, is shattered now and again as expresses on the London–Peterborough railway line flash by. Two more locks lead you to Godmanchester and – almost immediately – Huntingdon. The towns stand either side of a fourteenth-century stone bridge. Both are worth visiting. Godmanchester has a 365-acre (148-hectare) meadow, said to be the largest single hay meadow in England. **Huntingdon** has Oliver Cromwell's birthplace and the Cromwell Museum, formally the school which young Oliver attended. Samuel Pepys went to the same school some years later.

Houghton Mill, near Houghton Lock, is a seventeenth-century water mill owned by the National Trust, and open to the public in the afternoons from Saturday to Wednesday between April and September. Houghton Mill is mentioned in the Domesday Book, though the present brick and timber structure was built in the seventeenth century. Hemingford Grey's riverside church, near Hemingford Lock, has never been the same since a hurricane blew its spire off in 1741. The stump can be seen perched on the tower. St Ives' early fifteenth-century stone bridge, with six arches, has a chapel on it.

After Earith the river gets wider and becomes more exposed, flexing its muscles for its trek through Fen country to **Ely**. About 4 miles (6.4 km) short of the city is Stretham Old Engine, built in 1831 and still in working order. It is open to the public. It provided the power for a 37 ft (11 m) diameter scoop wheel which could lift 30,000 gals (136,200 l) of water a minute.

Ely Cathedral provides much to wonder at, likewise the chapel of King's School, dating back more than a thousand years. Hereward the Wake, the last Saxon leader to hold out against William the Conqueror, is believed to have sought sanctuary in the monastery, and to have been betrayed by the Abbot and killed.

Ely is an attractive, busy little market town. The flat, featureless Fens have a fascination for some people. If you're not one of them, take a good look at Ely, then turn for home.

Addresses

The Broads

General information

East Anglia Tourist Board,
Toppesfield Hall,
Hadleigh,
Suffolk IP7 5DN
Tel: 0473 822922

Brochures/reservations

Barnes Brinkcraft Ltd,
Riverside Road,
Wroxham,
Norwich, Norfolk NR12 8UD
Tel: 06053 2625/2333

Blakes Holidays Ltd,
Wroxham,
Norwich,
Norfolk
NR12 8DH
Tel: 06053 3221/2141

Hoseasons Holidays,
Sunway House,
Lowestoft,
Suffolk NR32 3LT
Tel: 0502 64991/62181

River Nene

General information

Anglian Water Authority,
Oundle Division,
North Street,
Oundle,
Peterborough PE8 4AS
Tel: 0832 73701

Brochures/reservations

Alvechurch Boat Centre Ltd,
Scarfield Wharf,
Alvechurch,
Birmingham B48 7SQ
Tel: 021 445 2909

Blisworth Tunnel Boats,
The Wharf,
Gayton Road,
Blisworth,
Northants NN7 3BN
Tel: 0604 858868

River Great Ouse

General information

Anglian Water (Cambridge Division),
Great Ouse House,
Clarendon Road,
Cambridge CB2 2BL
Tel: 0223 61561

Brochures/reservations

Annesdale Marine,
Riverside Boatyard,
Annesdale Dock,
Ely,
Cambs CB7 4BN
Tel: 0353 5420

Bridge Boatyard,
Bridge Road,
Ely,
Cambs CB7 4DY
Tel: 0353 3726

Ely Marina,
Babylon,
Waterside,

Ely,
Cambs
Tel: 0353 4622

Hermitage Marine Services,
The Bridge,
Earith,
Huntingdon,
Cambs PE17 3PR
Tel: 0487 840994

River Mill Boats,
School Lane,
Eaton Socon,
Cambs PE19 3HN
Tel: 0480 73431

River House Cruisers (base at Earith)
8 Market Passage,
Cambridge CB2 3QR
Tel: 0223 350777

West View Marine,
High Street,
Earith,
Huntingdon,
Cambs PE17 3PN
Tel: 0487 841627

WATERLUDE:
THE NATURALIST

Tony Howes

There are fewer hire boats on the Norfolk Broads now than there were twenty years ago. Although the holiday industry flourishes, the number of boats has dropped by about a third. The reason is the increased awareness of the need to protect and preserve the environment. The Broads Authority was set up, interested parties getting together, conscious that some sort of carefully planned control was necessary. They included farmers, conservationists, naturalists, water authorities, anglers, holiday operators, boat owners, residents and others. Legislation was brought in, and the Broads are now hailed as Britain's newest national park. Tony Howes, locally born and bred and knowledgeable about birds and wildlife, has an enviable position with Blakes, the oldest boat hire company on the Broads, founded before World War I. He welcomes the positive moves that are improving the Broads environment.

'People are thinking environmentally,' he says. 'As far as the boat owners are concerned, new hulls have been designed with low wash characteristics to keep down bank erosion.' There are signs of a return to sailing.

Tony Howes, with a background in public relations and advertising, began employment with Blakes nearly twenty years ago. His present post is manager, boating division. Blakes is a hiring agency for boats – cruisers, narrow boats and, in some regions, sailing craft – on canals throughout England and Wales, on the Rivers Thames, Severn and Avon, on the Scottish lochs, the Norfolk Broads, on Ireland's Rivers Shannon and Barrow and the Grand Canal, in Friesland and the south of Holland, on an extensive fiord in Denmark and the Mar Menor, virtually an inland sea, on Spain's Costa Brava.

Since 1989 the brochures have also featured Florida's St Johns River. The list of cruising grounds is constantly being extended. By now Belgium and possibly Yugoslavia may be included.

And the man who samples every one of them, who estimates whether a particular cruising ground is commercially viable for his company, is Tony Howes. What a way to earn a living!

'Yes,' he says. 'I've been on just about every waterway that we sell. But being in the holiday business, I can never get away for more than a week at a time.' The administrative side never lets up, but Tony concedes that it's not a bad life.

Getting on to waterways throughout Britain and overseas enables him to pursue his lifelong interest in birds and wildlife. Born in a village north of Norwich, he developed an enthusiasm for fishing at an early age. If the fish were slow in biting, he'd get distracted by the bird life around him, and learned to identify them.

He still fishes the Broads, often in the faster-flowing, unnavigable rivers where chub, grayling and trout can be found. The locals know where the big pike lurk – 20- and 30-pounders (9–14 kg). The British record pike was caught in the River Thurne.

'A lot of people probably have an interest in wildlife awakened by coming to the Broads,' says Tony. 'They see things they have never seen before. Here they see herons, coots and moorhens, the resident mallard, ducks that visit like shelduck and tufted duck. They see cormorants and crested grebe. Only a handful of hirers would be lucky enough to see a bittern, but more would probably hear one. They give a strange, booming call and live in the reed beds.

'Bearded tits are a distinctive little bird seen in the reeds. They have black markings on their cheeks. There's the more common reed bunting. We get marsh harriers and Montagu harriers and some birds of prey which hunt the marshes.

'Animals indigenous to the area are too exposed to visitor influence to be easily noticeable,' says Tony. 'The otter has disappeared, but the quiet observer has a chance of seeing the water vole, the tiny water shrew, frogs, toads, newts, grass snakes. Foxes and badgers are about. There are also "visitors" which have escaped from parks and settled happily in the wild. These include Chinese water deer and the tiny muntjac deer, and Egyptian geese with light brown coloration and striking red and greens on their heads.

'Cruising is a good way to see birds, and sailing particularly so, because most birds take little notice of the boats,' says Tony. 'A good pair of binoculars is useful. You shouldn't go for too high magnification because if you're looking for a bird in thick foliage or reeds you'll have a job to find it. A good field guide is essential. Read about which birds you are likely to see in a particular habitat. You also need to learn to identify bird calls. Get a butterfly and moth book, too. There are some interesting species around the Broads. The swallowtail butterfly is unique to this area. There's a brown dragonfly which is only found here.'

Cruising on the canals and rivers of Britain as well as the Broads, Tony sees many different birds. In Europe he has seen bee eaters, golden orioles and other exotic birds. On the St Johns River in Florida he and his wife have sighted ospreys by the dozen, bald eagles – and alligators. In Florida's cooler season, docile manatees, or sea cows, can sometimes be seen at the edge of the river.

'As in Britain, the wildlife aspect is very much part of the interest of a holiday for a lot of people,' says Tony.

IRELAND AND SCOTLAND

River Barrow, Bagnelstown, County Carlow

THE WATERWAYS OF IRELAND

The loughs of Ireland and lochs of Scotland provide a completely different type of inland cruising from the gentle canals and rivers of England and Wales. Part of their charm lies in their wonderful scenery and the freedom they allow to deviate from a narrow channel. Uninhabited islands which you can reach by dinghy and explore, and the flora and fauna that you rarely see elsewhere, are an added attraction.

Ireland

Northern Ireland (Lough Erne)

Where can you cruise amid green islands, moor and wander alone among mysterious early Christian images and monastic ruins? Where can you enjoy one of the best stretches of cruising water in Europe, 50 miles (80 km) long and up to 5 miles (8 km) wide – and with only one lock? Where can you find excellent restaurants, each with its own jetty, and order trout freshly caught from the very waters you are cruising? Where can you hire a luxury boat with a huge oval bed in its stateroom?

The answer each time is Fermanagh, the most westerly of Northern Ireland's six counties. About a third of County Fermanagh is covered by water, the largest mass being Upper and Lower Lough Erne, connected by the River Erne, on which stands the major town in the region, **Enniskillen**. That doesn't mean it's a city – the population is around 12,000. But it has excellent facilities for boaters: good free moorings, water points with hose provided, and right by the landing stage the Fermanagh Lakeland Forum, a superb leisure centre built with the aid of European Community funds. Holidaymakers can join in whatever's happening – swimming, archery, squash, basketball, judo, trampolining, weight training, tennis, keep-fit exercises with an instructor . . . Film shows and concerts are held there. Equipment can be hired. The Forum is open from noon to 10.30 pm on weekdays and on Saturday and Sunday afternoons.

Information on Enniskillen and the region is available at the Lakeland Visitor Centre. Be sure to ask about the Marble Arch Caves.

You'll see the Centre on your way to the shops, a short walk from the jetty.

When it comes to bars and restaurants, you're spoilt for choice. William Blake's bar in the High Street is probably the best known, with its bright red, Victorian shop front and pine-lined snugs up a wide stairway leading from the main bar. They sometimes place a shamrock on the creamy foam of your glass of Guinness and expect it to remain undisturbed on its frothy cushion when the rich black liquid has gone. Just up the road is the Crowe's Nest, a restaurant run by Jim and Cathleen Crowe, which has been in Jim's family for generations. On chilly days coals burn in the stone-built hearth which is at eye level when you're sitting down. After the banks close, you can change foreign currency at the Crowe's Nest. Imagine trying to do that in a small-town restaurant in England!

Enniskillen has a Watergate, an eye-catching twin-towered structure, much photographed from the river, which developed from a fifteenth-century castle. It houses the Fermanagh County Museum.

In spite of its recent tragic history, the town has a relaxed, friendly atmosphere. True, armed police patrol the streets, but their duties don't preclude them from having an amiable chat with the visitors. Military helicopters are active from time to time, flying low and fast around Upper and Lower Lough Erne. Otherwise all is tranquil. Don't let the Troubles prevent you from experiencing this beautiful cruising ground.

Two miles (3.2 km) downstream from Enniskillen is **Devenish Island**, on Lower Lough Erne, the site of a sixth-century monastery. An 80 ft (24 m) twelfth-century round tower with conical top rises magnificently amid gravestones and ruins which include a ghostly church of the same period. A trip boat from Enniskillen takes passengers to Devenish Island, so to savour the distant past and have it to yourself, go early or late – even by moonlight if possible. Windows face in four directions so the approach of enemies could be seen, and the door is 9 ft (2.7 m) above the ground, so the monks could dash in and pull up the ladder.

White Island, also on Lower Lough Erne, has stone effigies from even further back in history. Seven stone figures stand side by side against the wall of a roofless church. They have distinctively individual features. You first glimpse them staring at you in stony indifference as you walk from the jetty towards the archway leading to the church interior. No-one knows their history, but they have been dated as ninth- or tenth-century.

On **Boa Island**, which is accessible to both road and water traffic, in Caldragh Cemetery, is a grotesque pre-Christian idol with two faces. Awesome ecclesiastical ruins and ancient figures shrouded in mystery aren't the sort of marvels you see just anywhere. It's worth going to Lough Erne for these alone. Everything else is a bonus.

To return to the present day, the famous pottery at **Belleek**, by the River Erne, is an interesting place to visit.

Some say there's an island for every day of the year in the Fermanagh Lakes. The figure is probably nearer two hundred. Certainly they're not in short supply. Many are covered in long-established, dense woodland. Some are inhabited. Some are used for grazing cattle – the animals are transported on 'fenced-in' pontoons. Derelict houses – mansions, even – remain here and there. Wildfowl of many species are seen. Watch for golden plovers and kingfishers. Anglers in open boats lie up in the reeds and await the fish of their dreams. They may even land it, for this unpolluted water yields great catches. Tons are recorded at the big competition matches. An angler fishing purely for pleasure (or perch) may well find his day's catch totals more than 100 lbs (45 kg).

There are shallows to avoid, especially on Upper Lough Erne, and close attention must be paid to the chart. Navigation is no problem as the numbered marking system is first class. You need binoculars (probably provided) to see the numbers on the marker buoys as you approach.

The boat hiring companies all belong to the Erne Charter Boat Association to maintain high standards. To ensure that the loughs never get crowded, the number of hire boats available is limited to a hundred. Charlie Parkes, of Erincurrach Cruising, has prestigious Birchwood cruisers in his fleet, with interior fittings in teak and the aforementioned big oval bed. He has also introduced a cruiser purpose-built so that a disabled person can skipper it.

The hotels and restaurants around the lakes are also of a high standard. Close to Enniskillen, on Lower Lough Erne, is the Manor House Hotel, standing imposingly on a hill overlooking the water. One of the hire companies, Manor House Marine, is based here. On the Upper Lough, the Killyhevlin Hotel's restaurant is popular with locals and visitors.

Republic of Ireland

Ireland's three main navigable waterways are the River Shannon, the River Barrow and the Grand Canal, which links the two. All pass through splendid scenery, and the Shannon frequently bursts into lake form as though out of sheer *joie de vivre*. From Lucan on the Grand Canal, just outside Dublin, to the west coast where the Shannon spills into the Atlantic Ocean, are 124 miles (198 km) and 24 locks.

These uncongested navigations are among the least polluted in Europe. Eight hire fleets between them offer some 450 cruisers or narrow boats. A dinghy, chart and binoculars are standard equipment on the Shannon boats.

The Shannon is navigable for 137 miles (219 km), and tidal for the last 10 miles (16 km). There are only six locks. The river follows the course of history back to the days of the Vikings, with whom Irish chieftains fought for control. Remains of old monastic settlements can be seen. Many people start their Shannon cruise at **Carrick-on-Shannon**, which has some fine Georgian buildings. It is the river's leading resort town. Take time for a side trip through a succession of lakes and a shallow lock to Lough Key, with its wealth of wooded islands. There are forest walks amid giant cedars, oaks and beeches, and a bog garden. Back to Carrick and upstream this time to Leitrim and Drumshanbo, villages of some activity and splendid views on the way. Turn south, back through the now familiar Carrick-on-Shannon, to Jamestown where there are quiet moorings.

Narrows and wides alternate. Dense woodland, open reed-fringed water, little towns with supermarkets, good restaurants serving panfried salmon and pubs where impromptu music and singing, and amusing, sometimes baffling, conversations are struck up – all are typical of Ireland. You'll get a welcome – one hundred thousand welcomes, indeed – 'Cead mile failte'.

Hirers can go as far as Killaloe, on the southern tip of Lough Derg, though inexperienced boaters are advised to turn back on reaching Lough Ree. Both Loughs Derg and Ree are up to 20 miles (32 km) long and dotted with large islands. Careful navigation is required. At the southern tip of Lough Ree is Athlone, where the castle houses a museum. Athlone Lock takes you to the wide waterway towards Portumna. Stop on the way at **Clonmacnois** to see the most important monastic settlement in early Christian Ireland. The last high king of Ireland was buried here in 1198. On to Shannonbridge and some social life, and then to Shannon Harbour and the junction with the Grand Canal.

The river cruisers are not ideally suited to the canal, and vice versa, so if the canal appeals – as it does to many – you should vow here and now to make a return visit to the Republic, to hire one of the English-style narrow boats. From the Shannon the Grand Canal goes due west to Dublin. There's a hire base at **Tullamore**, a village renowned for Tullamore Dew whiskey and Irish Mist liqueur whiskey. Edenderry is a market town on a short spur. Going east, one of the last main centres before Dublin is the boating centre of Robertstown. Here is the junction with the River Barrow Navigation, which goes south to Waterford.

Interesting towns and villages on the route include **Rathangan**, a noted coarse fishing centre close to an ancient burial site, the Hill of Allen. **Athy** is a market town whose history goes back to medieval times, and sits at the junction of the River Barrow and an unnavigable section of the canal. The scenery is beautiful, with the Wicklow Mountains in the distant east. A Norman castle overlooks the Barrow at Carlow, where the river bridge is dated 1569. **Graiguenamanagh** is a photogenic town with the Duiske Abbey, founded in 1207, restored in recent years. It was the largest Cistercian abbey in Ireland. At the village of **St Mullins**, towards the end of the navigation, a monastery was founded in the seventh century, and the area has associations with early Celtic mythology.

If cruising in Ireland and conversing with its people doesn't slow you down and tranquillise you, as a holiday should, nothing will. The Irish have no time for Spanish mañana. They can't understand why any nation should be in such a hurry. The easy-going Irish always have time to chat and muse, and they love meeting visitors and telling them the tale. A lock keeper or passer-by may entertain you for an hour or two. There's no hurry. No queues are waiting at the lock. When did you last see another boat?

People wanting the Shannon experience without the responsibility of self-skippering can take an all-inclusive one- or two-week hotel barge cruise. There are also angling holiday cruises on a hotel barge, with all anglers' requirements catered for, including dinghies.

Visiting Ireland – the Province or the Republic – feels like going abroad, but mainland UK hirers have the added advantage of being able to take the dog. What mustn't be taken into the Republic is foodstuff – fresh or tinned meat, fish or dairy produce. The hire companies will provision your boat if you let them know what you want in advance. Boat hirers pay for the fuel as an extra. Don't forget it's pricey in Ireland. Allow £50–plus for diesel for a week's cruise.

If you're doing any fishing at all, you'll need a licence. The Irish Tourist Board will supply details.

Scotland

Loch Lomond, Loch Ness . . . Romantic names, romantic places. Loch Oich sounds less so, unless pronounced by a Scot. These waters, and more, are accessible to hirers, and while Loch Lomond – almost an inland sea – is considered more suitable for boaters with some experience, Lochs Ness, Oich and Lochy, conveniently linked by canal sections to form the Caledonian Canal, are all right for any responsible people hiring a cruiser for the first time.

Scotland's tourism infrastructure has improved enormously in recent years. On the boating scene, there are now more places to eat out, and to have a shower, and, to give access to them, more jetties and piers.

Cruising below Ben Nevis, Caledonian Canal

It is more than two hundred years since Thomas Telford provided canals between the three big lochs. The idea was to enable shipping to get from the West Coast to the North Sea. Today commercial sea-going vessels share the water with the pleasure boats. Even so, it is an uncrowded waterway. The Caledonian is 60 miles (96 km) long from Fort William to Inverness, comfortably cruised both ways in a week. The mountain scenery is spectacular. There are castles to visit, places to shop and eat out, forests to walk in, wildlife reserves, and game fish to catch. If you have no luck you can buy farmed trout and cook them on board. The ten locks used by hire craft are all manned, and the fees are included in the hire charge.

If you pick up your boat at Dochgarroch, near Inverness, you have the 23-mile (39 km) length of **Loch Ness** to enjoy first. About half-way along the Caledonian Canal you come to a stretch of cut with two locks and you are in a loch again – this time Oich, which doesn't have the awesome depth of Ness. Soon you are in the **Great Glen** region, where a geological fault wrenched mountain ranges apart millions of years ago. Great Glen Water Park is on the east bank.

Two more canal locks to **Loch Lochy**, at the foot of Britain's highest mountain, Ben Nevis. Banavie, at the loch's southern end, is the turning point, but take a look at the eight-lock flight called Neptune's Staircase that drops sea-going boats 64 ft (19 m) into tidal Loch Linhe.

Those who can't resist scenic railways can take time off the water for a train ride to Mallaig, on the West Highland Line, which includes the Glenfinnan Viaduct.

Thick forests, with a backdrop of mountains line the shores of **Loch Lomond**. It is 23 miles (39 km) long and 5 miles (8 km) across at its widest, and this region is dotted with islands, five of which are nature reserves. Scottish hand-crafted products can be bought at various outlets around the lake shores, and traditional Scottish hospitality is dispensed at restaurants and inns.

Fishing is prohibited on Sundays. Daily or weekly permits can be bought for other days. There are salmon and sea trout to be caught. Coarse fishing is free, and there is no close season.

Addresses

Northern Ireland – Lough Erne

General information

Northern Ireland Tourist Board,
River House,
High Street,
Belfast BT1 2DS,
Northern Ireland
Tel: 0232 31221

Northern Ireland Tourist Board,
11 Berkeley Street,
London W1
Tel: 01-493 0601

Brochures/reservations

Erincurrach Cruising,
Blaney,
Enniskillen,
Co. Fermanagh,
Northern Ireland
Tel: 036 564 507

UK Waterway Holidays,
Welton Hythe,
Daventry,
Northants NN11 5LG

Republic of Ireland

Note: Callers from outside Ireland should consult their telephone directory for area codes.

General information

Irish Tourist Board,
Ireland House,

150 New Bond Street,
London W1Y 0AQ
Tel: 01-493 3201

Bord Failte,
Baggot Street Bridge,
Dublin 2,
Ireland
Tel: 01 765871

Brochures/reservations

Athlonc Cruisers,
Jolly Mariner,
Athlone,
Co. Westmeath,
Ireland
Tel: 0902 72892

Blakes Holidays,
Wroxham,
Norwich NR12 8DH
Tel: 0603 784131

Carrick Craft,
PO Box 14,
Reading,
Berkshire RG3 6TA
Tel: 0734 422975

Celtic Canal Cruisers (Grand Canal),
Tullamore,
Co. Offaly,
Ireland
Tel: 0506 21861

Derg Line,
Killaloe,
Co. Clare,
Ireland
Tel: 061 76364

Emerald Star Line,
37 Dawson Street,
Dublin 2,
Ireland
Tel: 01 718870

Hoseasons Holidays,
Sunway House,
Lowestoft,
Suffolk NR32 3LT
Tel: 0502 501010

SGS Marine,
Balleykeeran,
Athlone,
Co.Westmeath,
Ireland
Tel: 0902 85163

Shannon Castle Line,
Dolphin Works,
Ringsend,
Dublin 4,
Ireland
Tel: 01 600964

Shannon Barge Line (angling hotel barge)
Main Street,
Carrick-on-Shannon,
Co. Leitrim,
Ireland
Tel: 078 20520

Shannon River Floatels,
Killaloe,
Co. Clare,
Ireland
Tel: 061 76364

Silver Line,
Banagher,
Co. Offaly,
Ireland
Tel: 0902 51112

Weaver Boats (hotel cruises),
Carrick-on-Shannon,
Co. Leitrim,
Ireland
Tel: 078 20204

Scotland

General information

Highlands and Islands Development Board,
Bridge House,
27 Bank Street,
Inverness IV1 1QR
Tel: 0463 234171

Scottish Tourist Board,
19 Cockspur Street,
London SW1Y 5BL
Tel: 01-930 8661

Brochures/reservations

Blakes Holidays,
Wroxham,
Norwich NR12 8DH
Tel: 0603 782919

Hoseasons Holidays,
Sunway House,
Lowestoft,
Suffolk NR32 3LT
Tel: 0502 501010

UK Waterway Holidays,
Welton Hythe,
Daventry,
Northants NN11 5LG
Tel: 0327 843773

WATERLUDE: CANALWARE PAINTER

Steve Radford in flippant mood

Steve Radford's boating days began when he was five years old and have continued ever since. His parents, living in Nottinghamshire, were bitten by the waterways bug after a relative bought a hull which needed fitting out, and Steve became similarly afflicted. His other great passion was painting. A few years ago, in his early twenties, he consolidated his twin interests and became a full-time self-employed painter of narrow-boat ornamentation.

'Every weekend in summer, and our holidays, were spent boating,' Steve recalls. 'But it wasn't enough. I wanted to live on a boat. I used to play with children who lived on boats, and I always had that dream.'

In 1985 the dream came true. To raise the money to make it happen, Steve worked first in an art studio specialising in textile printing, and then for several years painting identification marks and logos on the gleaming bicycles manufactured at Raleigh's Nottingham works. He was saving hard to buy a boat.

In his spare time he helped his father build a narrow boat in traditional style. His mother was rearing a baby owl which the family had found, so the boat was named *Owl*. (The fledgling survived and flew off to make its own way in the world.) The boat was 60 ft (18 m) long, suitable for cruising anywhere in the country except the Fens. Steve painted an owl on the boat's cratch board and added the traditional roses and castles on the cabin sides.

'I've been painting for as long as I can remember,' he says. 'I started canal painting when I was about sixteen. People said I ought to do it professionally.' After working all day at the bicycle factory, he would paint water cans, mugs, trays, handbowls, egg cups and small ornaments, accumulating enough stock to exhibit and sell at waterway get-togethers. His work was much admired, and orders began to come in. Soon he was being asked by people with newly acquired narrow boats to do the decorative painting. As time went on there were more orders than Steve could meet in his free time, and he said goodbye to the bikes.

His first 'studio' was Owl's stern cabin, which his father had built as an exact reproduction of a working boatman's cabin, and which Steve had decorated in mid-1800s style. His father, in the mean time, had built another narrow boat, and Steve took over Owl.

With the family's Jack Russell terrier, Pip, as his companion, Steve moved by water to where the work was. Pip became something of a waterways personality in her own right. Shortly before the IWA National Rally at Castlefield, Manchester, in 1988, she produced two unplanned pups, Josh, named after the Josher style of narrow boat, and Ricky, named after Rickmansworth boats. They kept Pip busy throughout the rally.

Steve's childhood cruising days were on the River Trent, when pleasure craft shared the water with oil tankers and other commercial traffic. In recent years the Trent has attracted more freight traffic, including gravel barges, especially in the tidal section.

Steve can usually be found at his stand at major waterway rallies and festivals, selling his canalware and taking orders for decorating narrow boats.

There seems to be no precise knowledge of the origin of this curious but cheerful and colourful art form. The castles are usually depicted as multi-towered 'fairytale' ones like those which dominate Rhineland scenery. Roses are not the only flower species represented. Designs include diamond-patterned borders, the four playing card suits, various symbols and assorted squiggles and blobs. They make up what is instantly recognisable as canal art. Practitioners develop their own style around a common theme. At one time a working boat's decoration revealed its canal of origin.

Strangely, there are few examples of early canal art in the waterway museums, most exhibits being from early this century. But it is good to know that a few professional artists like Steve are carrying on the tradition.

Address

Steve Radford,
5 Hillside,
Langrey Mill,
Nottingham NG16 4FT

FRANCE

Rochers du Saussois, Canal du Nivernais

France is riddled with navigable waterways, and almost anywhere a holidaymaker would wish to go by car can be reached by boat. Most people are aware of the Canal du Midi and the River Loire. They may know of the Marne or the Canal du Nivernais. But how many would know that there is wonderful cruising to be had in Alsace? Or that more than 420 miles (672 km) of cruising waters are waiting to be explored just across the English Channel in Nord-Pas de Calais, the French region closest to the United Kingdom?

There has always been something especially appealing about France as a holiday destination. Perhaps it's the wine. Certainly a large part of it is the food. Whatever it is is enhanced by the addition of water – and boats, of course. As with Britain, the waterways pass through the very best of the countryside, and from the deck of a *pénichette* (a purpose-built leisure cruiser modelled on the traditional French trading barge) or even a hotel barge you'll see places you would never have suspected existed if you'd been rushing along the autoroute by car.

Boating holidays have been available for years on the popular Canal du Midi and a few other waterways, but now even more opportunities are being offered by an ever-growing number of hire fleet operators. More British tour operators are beginning to include boating packages in their programmes. So let's start by taking a look at some of the areas and deals on offer.

The Package Deal Operators

Until recently, inclusive French waterway packages were largely in the hands of the two British leaders, Blakes and Hoseasons, with just a few small specialists selling directly to the public rather than through travel agents. Now, however, the competition is beginning to hot up, as both Blakes and Hoseasons will admit. The fact remains, however, that for the time being at least the giants still offer the greatest selection of boating holidays in Europe, and especially France, which takes the lion's share of the market.

Blakes, who claim they can arrange any kind of boating holiday anywhere for anyone, offer self-skipper cruising in six major areas of France: Brittany, Burgundy, Charente, Lorraine-Alsace, Maine-Anjou and Midi-Camargue. Craft range from stubby little plastic 'jelly moulds', accommodating two or three persons, and broad-beamed narrow-boat-style vessels of the type familiar on the English Broads, to some quite splendid steel-hulled craft you could sail across the Channel. The company also offer skippered barge cruising along the Canals Loire Latéral, Briare, Nivernais, Centre and Bourgogne in *La Belle Aventure* with accommodation for up to ten persons.

Hoseasons have a similar selection of waterways and a wider choice of boats. Their brochures strongly feature the relatively off-beat areas of Brittany, Anjou and Burgundy. A region only recently introduced to their brochures is Aquitaine, with cruising from Damazan along the Canal Latéral à la Garonne westerly to Castets-en-Dorthe and eastwards to Toulouse with such fascinating offshoots as the recently restored River Baize navigation to be explored on the way. Among the craft offered by Hoseasons is a very extensive fleet of the spacious Connoisseur Cruisers.

Abercrombie and Kent Travel, better known as tour operators dealing with some of the more exotic parts of the world, entered the boating holiday field with a range of professionally crewed hotel and charter barge cruises in various parts of France. At the top end of the scale is a nine-night holiday in the Loire region aboard the *Fleur de Lys*. Abercrombie and Kent claim it is the world's most luxurious canal and river barge, complete with heated swimming pool. With 1989 prices up to £5,059 per person the luxury would need to be unquestionable.

Eurocamp, a leader in the market for budget holidays under canvas and in mobile homes, struck out in a new direction in 1989 with the launch of a 16-page brochure offering canal cruising in six regions of France. The fleet consists of *pénichettes*, Connoisseurs and conventional cruisers. Prices when the programme was introduced started at £298 for four people sharing a boat for a week's cruise along the River Charente in the heart of Cognac country – less than £75 each and an indication of how reasonable a holiday afloat can be.

Flot'Home UK Ltd has a programme entitled 'Barge France' offering luxury cruising aboard three crewed barges in different parts of France: The *Stella Maris* in Alsace-Lorraine, *Anjodi* on the Canal du Midi, and the *Lady A* in Burgundy. The company places great emphasis on the good life – gourmet cuisine and stylish accommodation as the floating hotels glide through shady, tree-lined waterways in the heart of rural France.

French Country Cruises, a programme presented by London-based Andrew Brock Travel Ltd, offers *pénichettes* only. Accommodation below decks is spacious and there is more than average room on deck for sunbathing. This company is the only one we have found offering a starting base fairly near Paris – at Fontainebleau in the Ile de France. Bicycles can be rented – most useful for fetching the morning *baguettes*.

Just France, another small specialist operator, offers cruising in Burgundy, Alsace and the South of France and hotel boating on *Stella Maris*, *Anjodi* and *Lady A*. Cordon Bleu cuisine is the carrot, as it were, held out to tempt holidaymakers to try the barge holidays offered by the Saffron Walden-based specialist, Vacances. VFB Holidays, another upmarket specialist operator, goes for *pénichettes* only in its programmes based in Alsace, Burgundy and on the Midi.

Each of the companies mentioned above will make all travel arrangements, including reservations for ferrying your car across the Channel if required. Roughly speaking, it will cost about an extra £100 on top of the boat hire for four people and a car.

Rules and Regulations

As elsewhere in the world, vessels on French waterways should keep to the right, passing each other port (left) to port. Craft under sail and large commercial vessels have the right of way over pleasure cruisers, as do craft engaged in towing. The maximum speed limit on French canals varies from 3.6 to 4.8 mph (6–8 kph) and on rivers from 4.8 to 6 mph (8–10 kph). A good way of judging whether or not you are going too fast is to look back at your wash. If it is breaking you are certainly exceeding the speed limit. Slow down on bends and corners, when approaching bridges and when passing moored craft, dredgers, rowing boats, fishermen and swimmers. Hire craft should neither tow other craft nor be towed themselves without authorisation from the boatyard, which should be contacted as soon as possible in the event of a breakdown.

Locks on the French waterways are nearly always manned by a lock keeper. If you are approaching a lock at the same time as a commercial barge, observe the courtesy of the cut and let the professional in first. He (or she, very often) has a schedule to keep and a living to earn. On quieter canals in rural areas the lock keeper would appreciate a helping hand from the crew, who might well be glad of the chance to practise their French. Locks are open for traffic from 6.30 am to 7.30 pm between the beginning of April and the end of October. Out of season they open an hour later and close an hour earlier. They are very firmly shut during the sacred French lunchtime between noon and one o'clock each day throughout the year.

Some locks on the Canal Latéral à la Garonne are operated on a do-it-yourself electrical basis. They are simple to work, but you do need to know the procedure. Approaching the lock from either side you will see a cable stretched across the canal at a height of about 10 ft (3 m) from which a white pole dangles to within reach from a boat. This is the switch that works the lock. On the right-hand side of the canal there will be two red lights and two green ones. These are the traffic lights.

If two red lights are showing, tie up and wait for the next step.

If one green and one red light are showing, go to the pole dangling over the canal and move it a quarter turn to the right but do not pull it. Stay where you are and wait for the next step.

When two green lights are showing, move forward slowly towards the lock, entering only when the gates are fully open. If a red light is showing from the right-hand side of the lock itself, do not enter.

After tying up inside the lock go to the cabin ashore, outside which you will find a metal lever. Pull this to close the gates behind you. Wait for the water in the lock to rise or fall. Pull the lever a second time to open the gates ahead. You now have three minutes in which to get back on board and leave the lock before the gates close. Don't forget the crew as you sail away.

Canal du Midi

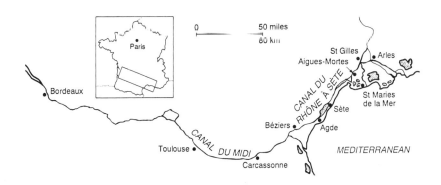

One of the best-known canals in the world, the Midi is part of a 370-mile (592 km) waterway system that extends from the Mediterranean to the Atlantic, avoiding a passage of 1,800 miles (2,880 km). It was the first section of the system to be built, astonishingly, more than three hundred years ago, although people had been thinking about the project since the times of the Romans.

The Midi was the work of Pierre Paul Riquet, still revered for his achievement by the people of Languedoc, for the canal brought not only improved communications and trade but also the water always so badly needed in this hot and arid area. The canal also brought a new splendour to the region, with its aqueducts, bridges – even its distinctive oval-shaped locks – matching the elegance of the Sun King, Louis XIV. Work on constructing the canal began in 1667 and ended fourteen years later. Riquet devoted the whole of his energy and fortune to the project and died, penniless, a few months before the triumphant opening of the Midi in 1681. It was the family of the 'Moses of Languedoc', as he came to be known, who benefited from the considerable profits the canal was soon producing.

Commercial traffic on the Midi today is negligible, but leisure traffic can be very heavy during high summer. However, there is plenty of cruising space: 160 miles (256 km), and only 65 locks, between Toulouse and Sète, with connections to the Canal Latéral à la Garonne to the west, the Canal du Rhône à Sète to the east, and the Canal de la Robine about halfway along the waterway. There is a good choice of starting points, but the bases favoured by British companies offering boating holidays in the area are at Agde, Castelnaudary, Colombiers, Homps, Port Cassafières, and Marseillan, with some starting at Beaucaire on the Canal du Rhône à Sète and Narbonne on the Canal de la Robine.

Shaded for much of its length by cypress, plane and pine trees, the Midi winds through sleepy old villages and walled towns, passing vineyards that extend beyond the horizon. Always charming, it is full of interest throughout its length and for much of the year adds the bonus of excellent weather, though mosquitoes can be a nuisance in June and September. Don't forget to pack the insect repellent. In general, provisions should present few problems – the canal passes through plenty of places with shops.

Climbing from Toulouse, the canal reaches its summit at Col de Naurouze. There, 620 ft (186 m) above sea level, a grand obelisk commemorates the achievement of the 'Moses of Languedoc'. From Castelnaudary, the Midi begins a gentle descent to the Mediterranean. Carcassonne, a medieval walled city, is well worth a visit. Below the lock at Argens the canal enters the **Grand Bief**, 32 miles (54 km) on the same level, the longest lock-free section on the French waterways system. Just above Colombiers, at the eastern end of the Tunnel de Malpas, you can moor the boat and climb to the Iberian-Greek hilltop city known as the **Oppidum d'Ensérune**. The view from here is stupendous. **Béziers** brings the double excitement of an inclined plane, built to replace a staircase of seven locks, and a graceful aqueduct crossing the River Orb, one of the first in the world built for navigation.

The Mediterranean begins to make its presence felt as the Midi descends from Béziers and passes through the vineyards of Corbières and Minervois as well as orchards of peach, apricot, plum and cherry trees. At Agde, now a popular playground, the canal enters the Etang de Thau, a great salt water lagoon renowned for its mussels and oysters. Across the lake is the picturesque port of Sète.

Canal du Rhône à Sète

With the Beaucaire branch and the Petit Rhône taken into account, the Canal du Rhône à Sète gives a total of 75 miles (120 km) of cruising waters, although some care is needed on the Petit Rhône because of mud banks. That might not sound like much of a distance, but the area is of full of excitement and the nearest thing to tropical boating you're likely to find in Europe, for the waterway takes you into the heart of the Camargue, that mysterious region of black bulls, white horses and thoughts of Vincent van Gogh.

Between Sète and the Crusader city of **Aigues-Mortes** the canal blends with many lakes and swamps teeming with wildlife: flamingoes, ospreys, rollers, hoopoes, marsh harriers, even beavers. The countryside, flat as only marshland can be, is set against a backdrop of the Cévennes and Alpilles mountains. Aigues-Mortes, with its thirteenth-century towers, was once located beside the sea, but silting over the centuries has made it into an inland city. A walk along the ramparts will give you a good view of the surrounding countryside. The area is covered by vineyards protected by yew hedges, and towards the sea huge piles of sea salt are set beside the marshes.

St Gilles, where the Beaucaire branch begins, is the gateway proper to the Camargue. From here you can also enter the Petit Rhône which winds south to the seaside town of **Les Saintes Maries de la Mer**, a place of pilgrimage especially for gypsies who go there to pay homage to their patron St Sarah. The town has several interesting old churches and is renowned for its religious festivals. Just above the city of **Arles** the Petit Rhône joins the Rhône river, which can be choppy and difficult when the hot Mistral wind blows against the current. Apart from its association with Van Gogh, Arles, a provincial capital in the time of the Romans, is worth visiting for its architectural treasures.

River Charente

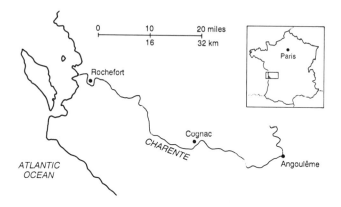

Situated in Cognac country, in south-west France, the Charente is navigable from Angoulême, to Rochefort near the river's mouth, a distance of just over 100 miles (160 km). Navigation was recently restored after a lapse of more than 50 years. The river has 21 locks, all but the last three to be worked by the boat's crew. There are two starting points for those hiring from Britain: St Simeux, not far from the upper limit of navigation, and Cognac. A week's easy cruise will take you from one base to the other and back and in both towns you can visit distilleries with famous names.

Angoulême has ramparts and a cathedral, and Saintes, downstream from Cognac, has Roman monuments and an ancient amphitheatre. Rochefort, a naval port and spa town, was built during the reign of Louis XIV. The region has many charming villages with Romanesque churches. The river has no commercial traffic and the water is clear and clean with excellent fishing and swimming – a splendid waterway for novices and the more experienced.

Waterways of Burgundy

Burgundy, the heart of France, is a superb cruising ground with a multitude of boating possibilities through countryside studded with ancient châteaux, vineyards and peaceful villages with tempting restaurants . . . No shortage of starting points here. The most popular are Auxerre, Chitry-les-Mines, Decize, Dijon, Gray, Joigny, Marseilles-les-Aubigny, St Jean de Losne, Tonnerre and Vermenton.

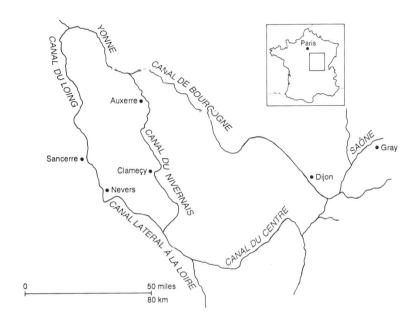

The Waterways of Burgundy

Starting from either Auxerre or Vermenton, boaters can cruise along the beautiful Canal du Nivernais and its mother river, the Yonne, through the hills of Burgundy on a waterway almost totally free from commercial traffic. A week's return cruise will include the large town of Clamecy, ancient stronghold of the Knights of Nevers. In a fortnight Châtillon en Bazois, with a beautiful château overlooking the canal, can be reached.

The Canal de Bourgogne links the navigations of the rivers Yonne and Saône and offers superb cruising possibilities. Heavily locked throughout its 150-mile (240 km) length, the canal is largely ignored by commercial vessels, and a blessing is that the locks are operated by keepers. Travelling south, it passes through the Côte d'Or and the centre of France's gastronomic arts.

Using the delightful town of Gray, on the River Saône, as a starting point offers a wide choice of routes. The Canal de Bourgogne, Canal de la Marne à Saône and the Canal du Centre are all within easy reach. This is the region for the wines of Beaune, Nuits St George, Chablis and Chambertin as well as Kir – and mustard – from Dijon.

Marseilles-les-Aubigny, an original canal village with houses surrounding the basin, is on the Canal Latéral à la Loire. A couple of days' cruising northwards leads to the noted wine area of **Sancerre**. The village is set at the top of a vine-covered hill and can be reached on foot (a moderately taxing walk) from the canal at St Thibaut – don't drop the bottle on the way back. Further north, at Briare, is the Pont Canal, an aqueduct over the Loire, which was built by Alexandre Eiffel, the man who built the tower in Paris. This marks the entrance to the Canal du Briare, France's oldest canal, completed in 1642. Southwards from Marseilles-les-Aubigny leads to Nevers by way of the combined lock and aqueduct system at Guetin, where the canal crosses the River Allier. Continuing past Decize leads to a short cruise on the Loire itself and on to the Canal du Nivernais.

Brittany's Criss-Cross Canals

Josselin, Brittany boasts a canalside fairy tale château

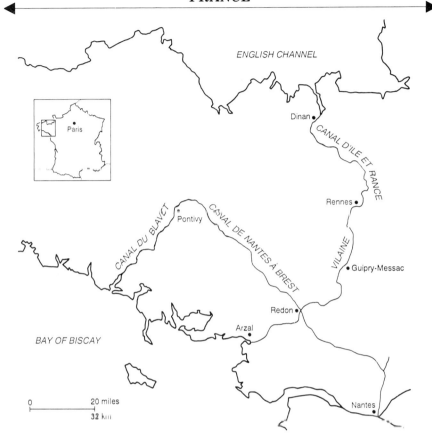

ENGLISH CHANNEL

Paris

Dinan

CANAL D'ILE ET RANCE

Rennes

CANAL DU BLAVET

Pontivy

CANAL DE NANTES À BREST

VILAINE

Guipry-Messac

Redon

Arzal

BAY OF BISCAY

0   20 miles
     32 km

Nantes

Brittany's major waterways form a neat cross over a map of the region, and they offer a very wide range of boating activities. With a total length of nearly 700 miles (1,120 km), they range between river, canal and sections so wide they look like lakes, so there is something for everyone – cruising, sailing, windsurfing, etc. There is virtually no commercial traffic.

Developed in the main by Napoleon to enable France to beat the effects of the English blockade at the beginning of the nineteenth century, the system was built up on the rivers Rance, Vilaine and Erdre. Today the Vilaine and the Canal d'Ile et Rance form a north–south leisure route between Dinan, not far from the English Channel port of St Malo, and Arzal, close to the Bay of Biscay. The horizontal arm of the cross, as it were, is formed by the Canal de Nantes à Brest with cruising from Pontivy eastwards towards Nantes and the Loire Valley. At the crossroads of the system is Redon where

French Country Cruises has a base. Other bases used by British hire boat companies are Arzal (Blakes and Eurocamp), Guipry-Messac and Dinan (Blakes).

As commercial traffic on the system declined this century its waterways fell into disuse and were soon showing signs of neglect. However, spirited prodding by the French Committee for the Promotion of Tourism persuaded local authorities to start restoration programmes, with commendable results. Although a number of hire boat companies now operate in Brittany, waterway traffic is still very light and it is rare to have to wait to pass through a lock.

Navigation throughout the system is simple with international traffic signs marking bridge arches and channels. Some stretches of the waterways are almost lock-free and others are quite heavily locked. There are numerous mooring places, many of them conveniently close to restaurants, shops and service points.

Even if you don't start your cruise at **Redon** you will certainly include it as a port of call. It's an attractive town with a well-protected yacht basin and some excellent restaurants. There are good shops and a street market is held each Monday. The cloistered church of St Sauveur has a fourteenth-century tower and other parts date from the eleventh and twelfth centuries. A cruise eastwards to **Josselin** will take a week. Josselin boasts a fairytale château right beside the canal and has some very picturesque seventeenth-century houses. Medieval **Dinan**, to the north with its ramparts and monuments, will mean a two-week cruise. The port of Dinan, about 250 ft (75 m) lower than the main town, is a charming spot with numerous restaurants and shops. Market day is Thursday.

South of Redon the Vilaine is lock-free to the the tidal barrage at Arzal. For hire cruisers this is the limit of navigation. Boaters starting from here can expect to get to Dinan and back in two fairly active weeks or to beyond **Rennes** and back in a week. Brittany's ancient capital, Rennes has a lovely old quarter rich in architecture dating from the Middle Ages. Much of the city was destroyed in a disastrous fire in 1720, but some of its most elegant streets were created as a result. **Pontivy**, a three-weeks' return cruise, stands at the junction of the Canal Nantes à Brest and the River Blavet and is set among some of Brittany's most picturesque countryside near Lac de Guerledan. Its position gave it a special strategic importance during Napoleonic times and for a time it was actually called Napoléonville. The town has a fifteenth-century château which is open to the public from mid-April to mid-October. Just outside Pontivy is the first of more than fifty locks that descend to Rohan in as many kilometres.

A leisurely fortnight's cruise from Arzal or Guipry-Messac will take a boat to **Nantes** and the junction with the River Loire. With a population of close on half a million, Nantes has plenty to offer tourists. Highlights are the castle of the Dukes of Brittany, the cathedral, botanical gardens and the Jules Verne museum.

Maine-Anjou

Three rivers – the Mayenne, Oudon and Sarthe – provide more than 150 miles (240 km) of cruising through some of the most tranquil countryside in France, a countryside dotted with lovely towns and villages, châteaux and abbeys, vineyards and old water mills. Throughout the whole system there are only 45 locks so getting

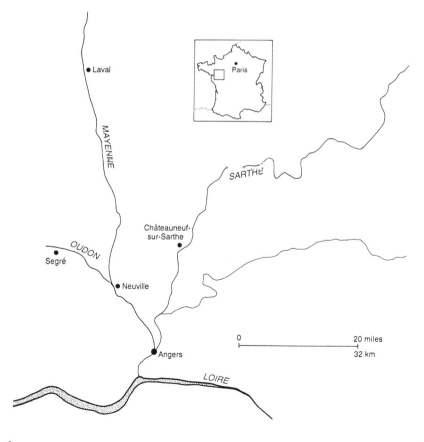

around is no problem – in fact it can all be done very comfortably in three weeks – from Laval on the Mayenne to Le Mans on the Sarthe Even a week's cruise would take you from, say, Chenille Change along the Mayenne to Laval and back, and in the same time you could do the return trip to Châteauneuf sur Sarthe.

The Mayenne, with 25 locks, winds through completely unspoilt countryside, and from Neuville you can take a detour along the Oudon to Sègre. The Sarthe has only twenty locks in its navigable length of 84 miles (134 km) and flows through many splendid old villages and small towns. Throughout the system there are good moorings, often close to superb restaurants.

Alsace-Lorraine

Growing rapidly in popularity, this is a great boating area, stretching from Strasbourg in the east to Vitry-le-François in the west and northwards to the West German and Belgian borders. Its waterways are the Canal de la Marne au Rhin, Canal de la Marne à la Saône,

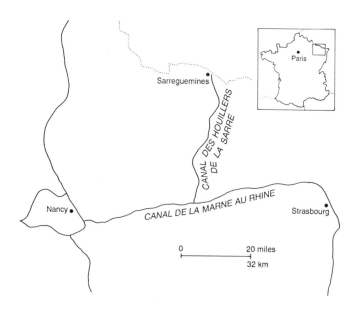

Canal de l'Est, Canal des Houillères de la Sarre and the rivers Moselle and Meuse.

Paradoxically for an area that has seen some of the worst violence in human history, has changed hands seven times in a period of 75 years and has been fought over three times in less than a century, Alsace-Lorraine is as peaceful a place as you would find anywhere on earth – especially on the water. Here are mountains, lakes and superb forests, towns steeped in history and attractive villages whose distinctive black-and-white half-timbered houses have drowsed through the centuries. For waterway buffs there are tunnels and an inclined plane – at Arzviller, near Lutzelbourg – which lifts boats 145 ft (43.5 m) and replaces 17 locks.

The main bases used by British operators are at Krafft, Lutzelbourg, Lagarde, Hesse, Sarreguemines and Toul. You could make a one-way trip between Krafft and Lagarde in a week, while a return trip in the same period would take you, from, say, Lagarde to Lutzelbourg and back. A one-way fortnight would take you from Krafft to Lagarde, with a trip up the Canal des Houillères de la Sarre as far as Sarreguemines included.

There are lots of interesting places to visit, of course. Close to the borders of France, Belgium, Germany, Luxembourg and Switzerland, **Strasbourg** houses the headquarters of the Council of Europe and the European Court of Human Rights and is the seat of the European Parliament. It is France's second largest river port. The city's grandiose cathedral took four centuries to build. The finishing touch – a single tower crowned with a spire – made it the tallest cathedral in France with a height of 461 ft (138 m). La Petite France, once the city's tanners' quarter, is a tastefully restored, traffic-free area of traditional half-timbered houses. Don't miss Les Winstubs, where you can enjoy a pitcher of Alsace wine in a convivial tavern atmosphere. Strasbourg has lots of museums, and every June the world-famous international music festival takes place. During the summer months a tourist information centre is set up on an old tug boat moored at the Quai des Pêcheurs on the River Ill.

Elegant **Nancy**, capital of the Duchy of Lorraine, is a welcoming place for boaters. There are plenty of moorings, and at Malzeville port water supplies and waste disposal facilities. The city has three distinct areas. The Old Town was founded in the eleventh century and includes the Old Palace, the Cordeliers Church in which the Dukes of Lorraine are buried, and the Craffe and Citadel gates. The area surrounding Stanislas Square was created by the Duke Charles III and reflects the finesse of eighteenth-century living in the grand style. The modern sector blends early twentieth-century town planning styles with the 'Nancy School', a bold architectural style characteristic of the new Europe.

From a leisure cruising point of view, you wouldn't expect much of a waterway called the Sarre Coal Mines Canal, but the Canal des Houillères de la Sarre is surprisingly unspoilt and lovely. There is little mining on the French side of the border. At its southern end, near its junction with the Marne-Rhin, the canal passes through an area which contains the largest concentration of lakes in France. Some have been given over to such leisure pursuits as swimming, sailing and windsurfing while others have become extensive wildlife sanctuaries. Throughout much of its length the canal passes through huge areas of forest in which deer and wild boar are to be found.

Nord-Pas de Calais

Amazingly, the region of France closest to Britain is the area least used by the hundreds of people who cross the Channel each year for boating holidays. Nord-Pas de Calais has a 425-mile (680 km) network of waterways in a region which has superb countryside, wonderful cuisine and towns and villages whose own history has helped to forge the British heritage. By boat you can visit such historically

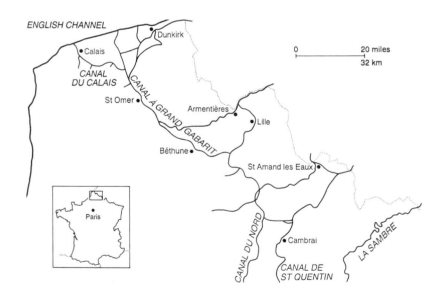

significant sites as the **Field of the Cloth of Gold**, reached from a branch of the Canal de Calais, where Henry VIII and the French king François I magnificently played power politics, and **Armentières**, on the River Lys, where more than 30,000 gas shells rained down during a ten-day battle in 1918.

Startlingly unoriginal, the local authorities have dubbed their region 'The Land of Canals', but it is a reasonable claim, for the system is both extensive and ancient. Waterways have been navigated here since the ninth century when coins were minted bearing the insignia of the very much inland port of Valenciennes. Vessels plied the River Lys between Armentières and Ghent in Belgium from at least the tenth century. In the twelfth century places like Lille, Douai, Bethune, St Omer, Dunkirk and Calais were able to make huge commercial strides because of the waterways.

Commercial traffic continues to play an important role today, and big cargo-carrying barges dominate the major routes. But determined efforts are being made to encourage leisure boating. The Association Régionale pour le Développement du Tourisme Fluviale Nord-Pas de Calais (Regional Association for the Development of Waterways Tourism) based at Armentières, works with state and local agencies on a continuing programme to develop cruising facilities. The work began in 1985, and the aim is to complete some sixty amenity sites over the next few years.

Facilities are already impressive. Three types of waterway amenity sites are provided: *halte*, *relais* and *base*, each with fixed or floating pontoons for moorings. A *halte* enables crews to stop for a few hours to visit local shops or attractions. Amenities include information, waste disposal and, sometimes, a picnic area. Overnight mooring is not permitted. A *relais* has similar facilities plus a slipway and, possibly, water and electricity supplies. Mooring is allowed up to several nights. A *base* is even more comprehensive, with repair facilities and on-site shopping.

The Waterways Association publishes attractive brochures providing information about the area, including concise descriptions of the canals and rivers, towns and villages, with details of boat rental companies and their fleets. Companies at Armentières and Wattignies, near Lille, offer craft accommodating from 4 to 12 people. None of the British operators has bases in the region at present, and there seem to be no plans for setting any up in the foreseeable future.

Canal de l'Ourcq

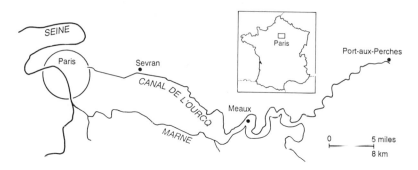

The Seine anywhere near **Paris** is no place for pleasure boating. The river is much busier with commercial traffic than the Thames in London and good, comfortable moorings are difficult to find. However, like London, Paris is blessed with a minor canal system ideal for small boat cruising.

There are three waterways: the Canals St Martin, St Denis and de l'Ourcq. The first two are both very short, providing access from the Seine for the Canal de l'Ourcq. All three canals are administered by the city of Paris, and charges are imposed for navigation. There is also a small fee for each lock negotiated.

Until recently there were no hire fleets operating in the area of Paris, but with recently relaxed regulations and authority's evident intention to encourage leisure boating, at least four companies now offer boats for hire.

The three canals link up at the Bassin de la Villette, close to the Jaurès Metro station, and there are shops and restaurants handy. Canal St Martin flows to the Seine at Quai Henri IV, near the Ile de la Cité. Nearly half of its 3-mile (4.8 km) length is in a tunnel. Canal St Denis connects with the Seine at St Denis, 4 miles (6.4 km) and six locks from the basin. The Ourcq travels more or less due east for 67 miles (107 km) to Port-aux-Perches. There are ten locks, five of them only 10 ft 6 ins (3.3m) wide, a fact that prompts aficionados to dub the waterway France's 'Narrow Canal'. Only one lock on the canal is operated by a keeper. The others are worked with a master key provided at the first lock.

For its first 12 miles (19 km) or so the waterway passes through light industrial and suburban areas, where there are facilities for boaters. After Mitry-Mory it moves into hilly countryside, and for nearly 18 miles (29 km) it runs very close to the River Marne. There is a proposal to build a boat lift near Lizy to create a long circular route from Paris.

Addresses

General information

Association Régionale pour le Développement du Tourisme Fluviale,
5/7 Avenue Marc Sangnier,
BP 46,
59426 Armentières,
Nord-Pas de Calais,
France

French Government Tourist Office,
178 Piccadilly,
London W1V 0AL
Tel: 01-491 7622

Brochures/reservations

Abercrombie & Kent Travel,
Sloane Square House,
Holbein Place,
London SW1W 8NS
Tel: 01-730 7795

Blakes Holidays Ltd,
Wroxham,
Norwich NR12 8DH
Tel: 0603 784131

Andrew Brock Travel Ltd,
10 Barley Mow Passage,
London W4 4PH
Tel: 01-995 3642

Eurocamp Canal Cruising,
Edmundson House,
Tatton Street,
Knutsford,
Cheshire WA16 6BG
Tel: 0565 3844

Flot'Home UK Ltd,
22 Kingswood Creek,
Wraysbury,
Middlesex TW19 5EN
Tel: 078481 2439

Hoseasons Holidays Abroad,
Sunway House,
Lowestoft,
Suffolk NR32 3LT
Tel: 0502 500555

Just France,
1 Belmont,
Lansdown Road,
Bath BA1 5DZ
Tel: 0225 446328

Vacances Ltd,
22 Gold Street,
Saffron Walden,
Essex CB10 1EJ
Tel: 0799 25101

VFB Holidays Ltd,
1 St Margaret's Terrace,
Cheltenham,
Gloucestershire GL50 4DT
Tel: 0242 526338

THE
NETHERLANDS

This lift bridge is a landmark in Amsterdam

The Netherlands, segmented by 6,000 miles (9,600 km) of navigable waterways, is a country made for boating. In Amsterdam, it seems impossible to take more than a few paces without finding oneself at the water's edge, and the city has more than a thousand bridges crossing its jigsaw puzzle of canals.

Water constitutes a fifth of the country's total area, and the Dutch have put it to good use. Goods of all kinds are conveyed by vessels ranging from huge barges carrying whole fleets of new cars to skiffs selling local produce along the backwaters of the smallest villages. Craft flying the flag of the Netherlands are seen on waterways throughout Europe. We even found a Dutchman doing business as a floating fishmonger, selling herrings from a clog-shaped wooden boat at Oudenaarde in Belgium, not far from the French border.

It follows, naturally, that the Dutch are a nation of superb sailors, handling their beautifully maintained boats with consummate ease, nonchalantly nudging with a knee the tiller of a 100 ft (30 m) long barge as it progresses along a busy, narrow canal *under sail*; or squeezing a 30 ft (9 m) motor cruiser into a mooring space you'd have thought tight for a craft half the size. It can all be rather daunting for the casual boater, to say nothing of the novice, and you can feel conspicuously foolish when something goes wrong. But the Dutch are discreet spectators. They watch with expressionless interest and say nothing, although they can be extraordinarily generous with help and encouragement if you indicate you need either or both.

The Dutch are also born linguists, so it is a good idea to fly your own Union Jack, Maple Leaf, Stars and Stripes, or whatever, to show that you would be glad if they spoke to you in English. They will be only too pleased to do so.

With all that water, cruising is possible almost everywhere, but the most popular area for those hiring boats is Friesland, in the north, where a labyrinth of canals, some hardly more than ditches, wriggles and weaves across a landscape *exactly* how you always imagined Holland to be. It is very, very flat, and there is a windmill in every view. There is the bizarre sight of yachts and sailing barges apparently gliding across open fields. The waterways of Friesland frequently spill out into meres – vast expanses of water where the wind can sometimes create open-sea conditions.

Only experienced yachtsmen are allowed to take chartered vessels into the Ijsselmeer and Waddenzee, and then only when the wind is less than Force 6. But in general the waterways of Friesland are very safe, even for novices, and in any event, boat-rental operators will always make sure that skippers and crews are well briefed and properly instructed before setting out.

The only licence you might need on the waterways of the Nether-lands is a fishing licence. There are no tests to pass, no certificates of competence to show, before you can take charge of a rented boat.

Whether you rent a modern cabin cruiser or a traditional round- or flat-bottomed boat with lee boards and a large area of sail, the craft is certain to be well equipped. It is likely to have two toilets and two showers. Some companies do not supply bedding, but will rent sleeping bags for a nominal sum.

With enough time to spare, you could explore most of the Dutch waterways in a season, but most people have only one or two weeks, so it's a good idea to plan well ahead and decide which area is best suited to the interests of the crew, bearing in mind that much greater distances can be covered each day than on UK waterways

For peace of mind, it's best if small cruisers avoid the big commer-cial arteries. Some of the barge traffic really is massive.

Decide which places you want to visit, and map out a route accord-ing to whether you want to go as directly as possible or divert to take in some extra sightseeing or browsing.

Navigation

Make sure you have charts for the regions you plan to cruise. The charts give a lot of information on water depths, buoys, bridge heights and widths, locks and distances. Information on where to obtain them is available at offices of the Netherlands Board of Tour ism and any one of the four hundred local tourism information cen-tres throughout the Netherlands should be able to help. Look for the VVV sign. Rental craft should have the appropriate charts on board.

Some people might welcome the fact that locks are few and far between in a land where some canals are actually *below* sea level. Bridges are another matter. Make a note of the height of your craft above the waterline in metres. On a rented boat this will be found in the literature provided. Most bridges display a board showing headroom, and swing bridges and lift bridges also announce opening times – they are usually closed for a lunch break – and the toll required. Locks are mostly free. Lock chambers are large, but easily negotiated. The lock keeper will indicate where he wants you – and if you are relegated to the back in a full lock with several barges, then tough luck. You'll need to keep back from the barrage of water churned up by those big screws as the powerful barge engines surge to leave the lock.

The charge made at movable bridges is modest, and in towns there is usually a single charge to cover several bridges. Bridge keepers 'fish' for tolls by dangling a wooden clog on a rod and line. You or your crew put the money in the clog and it is hauled away. Always keep a supply of small change handy by the helm.

Rules and Regulations

Most movable bridges are controlled by a system of lights. Two red lights mean the bridge is closed. If there is a red light on either side of the bridge, give three long toots on your horn. When one light is red and the other is green prepare to go through. Two green lights mean you can go ahead. If the bridge opens but two red lights remain on, hold off for a minute – another vessel is coming through from the opposite direction.

The same lighting system applies to locks. It isn't customary to tip at locks or bridges. The speed limit is 5–6 mph (9 kph), and slower on narrow canals.

Commercial traffic has priority over pleasure craft, and the lock staff know exactly the order in which they want the lock occupied, so be prepared to do as you are told, and be patient. If you are working to a deadline – returning your boat to the hirer, perhaps – you should have a rough idea of how long it will take you to get through any locks and complete the journey.

Moving bridges, however, can be less predictable, and you should allow for these. If you've just missed a bridge opening you may have to wait for other craft to catch up with you, or approach from the other direction, before the bridge keeper considers it worth while stopping the road traffic again. This happens particularly at rush hour ashore. If you have the misfortune to arrive just after the keeper has gone for his lunch the only answer is for you to do the same. On board you should have a note of bridge opening and closing times. In some places your superstructure may be low enough for you to get under some of the bridges, anyway.

Space permitting, you can moor outside taverns and restaurants, and in town and village centres. Visitors are also welcomed at marinas and sailing clubs. There will be a small mooring fee to pay. Many free moorings are to be found along rural sections of the waterways.

Western Holland

Amsterdam

Capital of the Netherlands and the centre of culture, Amsterdam is divided into neat little 'sub-zones' by a network of canals crossed by more than a thousand bridges. The city has at least 60 art galleries, 40 museums, 30 theatres and a dozen concert halls, as well as a fine range of architecture and an entertaining red light district which is probably one of the world's top tourist attractions.

To tour the city properly, it's probably a good idea to moor your boat and let someone else do the driving. *Rondevaarts*, the big, glass-topped trip boats, offer interesting canal excursions, or you can be independent and go by underground railway after deciding on your priorities. Tourists can buy a combined ticket covering train, boat, tram, metro and bus trips for a day.

Through the Bulbfields

People choosing an April or May holiday will want to see the bulb-fields of western Holland, which provide stunning swathes of vivid colour. The canal route to the south of Amsterdam and towards the Hook of Holland passes through this region, and boats from 2 to 12 berths can be rented from yards on the Amsterdam-Rijnkanaal between Amsterdam and Utrecht.

The Ringvaart Kanaal, to the south-east of Amsterdam, also passes through vast bulbfields. **Aalsmeer** is home of the world's biggest flower auction. The sales take place between 7.30 and 11.30 am. Many of the flowers and pot plants are delivered by boat – a sight to lift the spirits. Not far from here, a short side branch leads to Lisse and the famous Keukenhof Gardens, said to be the greatest flower show on earth. There are millions of tulips and other spring flowers in the 70-acre (28-hectare) park, which also has 5,000 sq. yds (4,180 sq. m) of glasshouses.

Haarlem, a little to the north-west of Amsterdam, on the Noordzee Kanaal, is also in bulb country, in an area favoured by the seventeenth-century Dutch painters. Frans Hals, of *Laughing Cavalier* fame, spent his final days here in an old people's home which is now a museum housing his work.

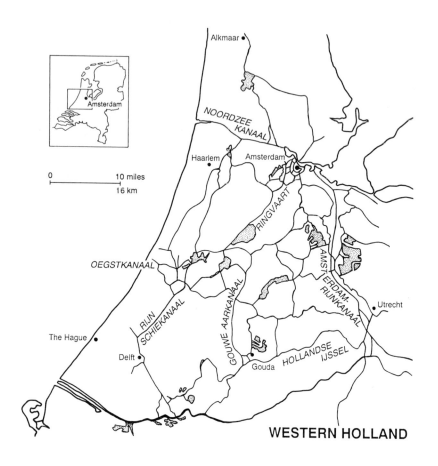

WESTERN HOLLAND

Cheese and Beer

Continuing northwards, along the Noordhollandsch Kanaal, among more tulip fields, you come to **Alkmaar**, and if you can arrange to be there on a Friday morning between the end of April and mid-September you'll see the Cheese Carriers Guild in action.

Thousands of shining spherical cheeses are brought on sledge-like barrows by white-clad carriers who wear lacquered straw hats coloured red, green, yellow or blue to match the barrows and denoting which of four companies they belong to. In a ceremony nearly four hundred years old, the cheeses are weighed, tasted, crumpled to test their fat and moisture content before being sold amid clapping of hands. There is a Cheese Museum in The Weighhouse, which dates from 1583 and has a carillon that plays folk songs on Friday mornings.

Alkmaar's National Beer Museum De Boom is housed in a seventeenth-century building that was once a brewery. A maltster, brewer and cooper can be seen demonstrating their skills, and in a bar in the basement you can sample some of the 86 types of Dutch beer.

Utrecht

Holland's fourth largest city after Amsterdam, Rotterdam and The Hague, Utrecht is capital of the province bearing the same name – a province with rare undulations, country houses, castles, big estates and rolling parkland. A former Roman citadel, the city is on the Merwede Canal, close to the Old Rhine (Oude Rijn), claimed by devotees to be the loveliest waterway in the Netherlands. Other waterways, including the Amsterdam-Rijnkanaal, wind about the city, which has streets of high gabled houses, historic buildings and old monuments. The Dom Tower, all that remains of a cathedral, is more than six hundred years old and at 367 ft (110 m) high a landmark hard to miss. It has three ornate, balconied levels – two of them square and one octagonal.

Travelling west towards Gouda, along the Hollandse Ijssel, brings us to **Oudewater**, where it is worth going ashore to see some splendid medieval architecture. This is the main route, between Utrecht and Rotterdam, busy with barges and not for the inexperienced who would be wise to miss Oudewater and reach **Gouda** via the Schiekanaal or one of the many minor waterways to the west of the Amsterdam-Rijnkanaal.

Gouda is a town for strolling in, with lovely shops and decorative buildings. Its Cheese Market is open on Thursday mornings during the summer. The fifteenth-century Sint Janskerk (Church of St John) is the biggest in the Netherlands – 403 ft (123 m) long – and has priceless stained-glass windows dating from the sixteenth century.

Delft

The towns in this green-belt region become ever more attractive. Beautiful Delft, at the junction of the Rijn Schiekanaal and the Delftse Schie, has narrow canals lined with trees and crossed by pretty white bridges. Its sixteenth-century buildings, its squares, sidewalk cafés and courtyards can be viewed from a horse-drawn streetcar.

Delft has a flower market, Saturday flea markets – some of them on the canals – and, on Thursdays, a general market where strect organ music harmonises – or perhaps not – with a carillon in the tower of the New Church, which actually goes back to the fourteenth century. The Old Church, which has a slanted tower, dates from the thirteenth century. They have long and precise memories in Delft.

The town's best-known product is its blue chinaware, still made by hand. De Porceleyne Fles, the royal Delft ceramics factory, and other ceramics workshops are open to the public.

Rotterdam and The Hague are each within a short distance of Delft, in opposite directions. Rotterdam is a huge seaport, with shipping and commercial barge traffic to match, and finding a mooring would be difficult. Better, perhaps, to go by public transport. The city has been rebuilt since World War II, when it was virtually flattened, apart from the Delfshaven area of twisting streets and houses of the seventeenth century.

Boat trips around Rotterdam harbour start from Wilhemsplein quay. Don't miss the view from the 600 ft (180 m) high Euromast. They say that on a clear day you can see for 33 miles (53 km).

The Hague

Queen Beatrix of the Netherlands lives in The Hague, which is the country's seat of government and home of the International Court of Justice. Gracious old buildings, parks and gardens, avenues and boulevards, pedestrian precincts and small canals contribute to a relaxed ambiance unusual in a big city.

Works by Rembrandt, Rubens, Van Dyck, Vermeer and Holbein can be seen at the Mauritshuis Museum located in a building dating from the mid-seventeenth century. Modern art can be seen at the Geemeente Museum.

Few visitors to The Hague would want to miss **Madurodam**. It is a typical Dutch town, with gabled buildings, market stalls, trains and windmills. What makes it untypical is the fact that everything is scaled down to 1/25th of its real-life size. There are accurate models of famous buildings in the Netherlands, and Madurodam provides a lesson in local government, as well as entertainment, for local schoolchildren who stand for election as mayor and councillors.

Open from the end of March to late October, the model city honours one of The Hague's heroes of World War II, a young Hussars officer named George Maduro, whose courage saved lives during the 1940 invasion of Holland. He died in Dachau concentration camp in 1945.

If you rented your boat from one of the yards south of Amsterdam – and you have enough time – you could make your way due east of the Hague to complete a triangular route and take in **Arnhem**, the city devastated in 1944 and rebuilt. The tragedy of those dark days is recounted at the Airborne Museum. The Kröller Müller Museum has the world's largest collection of Van Gogh's paintings – more than 250 of them – and some by Picasso.

Friesland

The best cruising and sailing waters in the Netherlands are in Friesland. There are many towns to visit, and there are also mile upon peaceful mile of canal, river and mere where there are few signs of human habitation. Gregarious crews looking for action in the evenings should plan their routes carefully.

Many of the waterways see little commercial traffic, so it is a pleasantly relaxed region where you can find time for a spot of fishing or sunbathing. Photographers and birdwatchers will be kept busy.

A word of caution. Some of the meres in Friesland are like inland seas and can become quite choppy when the wind gets up. Crew members moving about on deck should wear life vests, which should be provided on request by the boat hire company.

Channels through these stretches of water are clearly marked with buoys, but charts should be closely studied before the start of a voyage and the skipper should know which sectors are closed to motor boats, where the bridges are and whether they are fixed or non-fixed, and any other details affecting navigation.

The region's thirty lakes and many interconnecting canals and rivers are all on one level, so there are no locks to impede progress. It's amazing how much of the map can be covered in a short time –

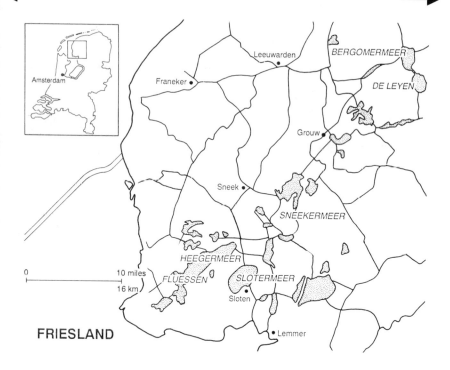

FRIESLAND

even keeping well below the speed limit. There is such a wide choice of routes that there is little need to cover the same water twice.

The people of Friesland have an independent spirit. They have their own dialect – a separate language almost – and they seem to regard their province as a separate country. But they are just as friendly as other Dutch people.

Friesland's capital is **Leeuwarden**, on the Van Harinxma Kanaal. It stands on hilly ground – the hills are man-made on reclaimed land. Leeuwarden is an old city with many sixteenth- and seventeenth-century buildings. Mata Hari, the dancer and courtesan, was born here and there is a statue of her in the city.

Sneek

Sneek, Friesland's second town, is a popular yachting centre, and the scene of an exciting sailing race during 'Sneekweek' every August when fully-rigged traditional Dutch craft are put to the test. Home

Watergate, Sneek – at the centre of the Friesland broads

of the Friesian Nautical Museum, Sneek is a picturesque town with a twin-towered seventeenth-century watergate, the only remaining part of the town's defence system.

Sneek's main bridge – one of three lift bridges in the town – is wide and busy. A single toll dropped in the bridge keeper's clog covers vessels for the other two bridges, too. There are good moorings close to the town centre, and in the evenings residents and visitors stroll along the quayside. There is a charge of a few guilders, depending on the boat's overall length, for using the town moorings. When the fee is collected you will be handed a carrier bag containing balloons, a few sweets and some brochures – a nice public-relations touch.

The bad news about these moorings is that Sneek's youth marching band rehearses on some evenings in the nearby cattle market. Musically, they are not bad, but the sound can be a bit maddening.

A few miles south of Sneek is **Woudsend**, where a small church has been cleverly converted into a restaurant. There are some pleasant waterside taverns where you can sit outside with a lunchtime drink and a snack while waiting for the bridge keeper to return from his lunch.

Sloten

Just south of Woudsend is Slotermeer, a wide open stretch of water where two waterways, the Luts and the Slotergat, converge. The Luts leads into Western Friesland and ultimately to such places as Workum, Bolsward and Franeker. The Slotergat, the eastern exit from the mere, leads to Sloten, said to be Holland's smallest town, with a population of 700.

Sloten, a charming place to wander around – though it won't take long – has two or three good restaurants and is well worth an overnight stop. Waste disposal and water are available at the main moorings, alongside the town's public car park, which is a lot quieter than you might expect. There is a small charge for overnighting here, or you can moor free farther along the canal.

A narrow waterway goes through the centre of the town. From the wooden footbridges which cross it, you may see an elderly couple out in their rowing boat, or youngsters paddling canoes. Dutch families in larger craft may have moored for supper in the shadow of the windmill which stands on old fortifications.

If you plan to eat out in Sloten, don't leave it too late. The restaurants may close early, especially in early or late season. Provisions can be bought at a small supermarket – which can easily be missed – and at a couple of bakers and a butcher's shop.

Lemmer

Lemmer, on the Ijsselmeer, is another popular cruising centre. Yachting Sirius, a member of Hoseasons' marketing consortium, rents out the Connoisseur craft developed originally for the Norfolk Broads. To get from the company's boatyard to the Stroom Kanaal, or vice versa, you have to negotiate a few hundred yards of the Ijsselmeer, a voyage excluded from the restrictions mentioned at the beginning of this chapter. Yachting Sirius has turned its hangar-like building into a good landmark by painting the Dutch tricolour on one huge door and the Union Jack on the other.

The Stroom Kanaal is entered through the only lock likely to be encountered for days. It takes you *down* to the level of the inland waterways, and it presents no difficulty as long as your lines are secured round the chain that extends the length of the lock wall – or send someone ashore to put them round the bollards.

The fee paid to the lock keeper also covers you for three lift bridges which have to be negotiated before an audience of experienced young sailors of both sexes enjoying drinks outside waterside cafés and bars. Don't be unnerved by this – their laughter is almost certainly the result of some other stimulus.

Lemmer is a busy little town, and central moorings may all be occupied, but there are good ones a short distance away, and it is a pleasant walk into town past boats from many ports.

Prinses Margriet Kanaal

The Stroom Kanaal leads into a big mere, Groote Brekken, and the busy Prinses Margriet Kanaal, which goes almost in a straight line to Koevordermeer. The route through is clearly marked by buoys. There is a choice of routes to the west, but the time comes when you have to choose between going west to Sneek or remaining with the Prinses Margriet Kanaal into the expanse of Sneekermeer and on to Grouw, a mid-Friesland regatta town, or following the major waterway to Groningen, not far from West Germany, if you have the time.

Keep your eye open for landmarks when navigating through Sneekermeer. It's easy to get disorientated in the maze of southern channels, which includes one or two dead ends. The sight of a heron catching a fish can make you miss your turning.

Coastal Towns

The route to west Friesland, via Slotermeer and the Luts waterway, passes through lovely wooded scenery and leads to a number of towns on the Ijsselmeer coast.

Hindeloopen, a picturesque little place with a strong Scandinavian influence, is famous for its painted furniture, now only to be found in the museum. North of Hindeloopen, and a mile or so inland, is **Workum** which supplied eels to London for hundreds of years. Its town hall dates from the fifteenth century. **Makkum** is noted for its pottery. Its villagers claim it is better than Delft ware. East of Makkum is **Bolsward**, one of Friesland's oldest towns, with a church built in 1446.

The seaport of **Harlingen** has a wealth of gables, built between the seventeenth and nineteenth centuries. Most of the centre of the town is preserved, and parts of the old fortifications can be seen. Fishermen bring mussels and shrimps into the port. The Van Harinxma Kanaal links Harlingen with **Franeker**, in north-west Friesland.

A man called Eise Eisinga lived in Franeker in the eighteenth century, earning his living as a wool comber. But he wanted to be an astronomer, and in 1774 he began to convert his living room into a planetarium. It took him seven years, and it operates to this day. It is open to the public during the summer.

North of Franeker, by going either through or round Leeuwarden, you can join the Dokkummer Ee, leading to Dokkum in northern Friesland. It is a long and fairly uneventful waterway, so perhaps the crew will welcome a diversion to the hamlet of **Hoogebeintum**, east of Dokkum, to see the highest mound in the province. They are unlikely to suffer from altitude sickness. The mound, a refuge from floodwater in the past, is 35 ft (10.5 m) above sea level.

Addresses

General information

Netherlands Board of Tourism,
25–28 Buckingham Gate,
London SW1E 6LD
Tel: 01-630 0451

Brochures/reservations

Blakes Holidays Ltd,
Wroxham,
Norwich NR12 8DH
Tel: 06053 3221/2141

Hoseasons Holidays,
Sunway House,
Lowestoft,
Suffolk NR32 3LT
Tel: 0502 500555

Yachting Sirius BV,
Vuurtoronweg 15,
8531 HF Lemmer,
Netherlands

BELGIUM

Historic Bruges offers picturesque boating

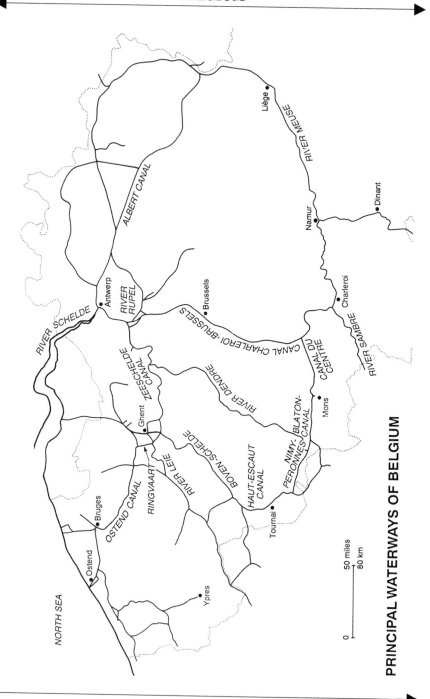

PRINCIPAL WATERWAYS OF BELGIUM

The Belgians have 1,250 miles (2,000 km) of navigable rivers and canals, and have so far failed to see them as a leisure boating facility. But thanks to commendable individual enterprise, it is now possible to rent cabin cruisers in Ghent and at a base in the south on the River Sambre.

Two separate companies, recognising the potential of the waterways as holiday cruising areas, have launched hire fleets and are out to attract holidaymakers from Britain, France, the Netherlands and West Germany

Belgium's waterways are efficiently maintained for commercial traffic, which is pretty heavy on most of the system, but at present facilities leave a lot to be desired for the visitor afloat – except in towns.

Canal towns like Ghent, Mons, Tournai and many smaller ones have central moorings, interesting places to visit, shops, bars and a wide choice of restaurants and cafés, but there are few convenient moorings between the towns. Frustratingly, there are many lovely rural stretches of water, but it can be difficult finding a suitable and safe place to tie up. There are many places where bollards are provided, but they are meant for barge traffic and are set too far apart to be of much use to the average pleasure craft.

Some Hazards

Using mooring spikes can be hazardous in busy commercial waterways. On much of the system the gradually sloping banks are fortified with rocks strewn at the waterline. A passing barge sucks away a lot of water and can leave a small craft in danger of grounding, whether it is moored or under way near the bank. Sometimes five or six barges will go by in as many minutes. Furthermore, the mooring spikes, even hammered in to the hilt, will be loosened, if not pulled right out, by the suction of huge, heavily laden barges rushing along to reach a lifting bridge or lock before it closes for the night.

The barges have to slow down in towns, of course, but outside they can cause a tremendous wash. Some steerers courteously reduce speed for pleasure craft, but many barge on, so to speak, putting glassware and crockery, if not life and limb, at risk.

You can find safe moorings, not too near a bend, and with something secure and handy to tie up to, but the chances are you'll be a fair way from civilisation, facing the prospect of another evening of Scrabble – if a barge hasn't already scattered the tiles. Occasionally, you may find a small yacht club – these are becoming more prevalent – and visiting craft are welcomed if there is space available.

Most villages are a mile or so from the waterways. Green Waterway Holidays, which operates a fleet of cruisers from Ghent – the company is based in Bruges – thoughtfully provides a couple of bicycles with each craft, so it's easy to go in search of food, drink and new faces.

We don't mean to knock Belgium. The country is small and compact, and there is usually a town within easy cruising distance. Many are historic centres, with attractive old streets and stunning art collections.

You see the occasional Dutch, French or German flag on yachts and pleasure craft using Belgium waterways, and the Belgians themselves are just beginning to appreciate the idea of getting afloat. Commercial barge traffic no longer has the system almost entirely to itself.

Waterway Giants

Belgium has some deep, wide waterways, with formidable barges to match. Most carry at least one private car on the deck, and possibly a motor cycle as well. Every barge has a square 'bungalow' at the stern in which the wheelhouse as well as the spacious family accommodation is situated. Big armchairs, lace curtains and a profusion of ornaments make it as cosy as any land-based home.

Often these giants are crewed by only two people – a husband-and-wife team – with the skill to steer the barge exactly where they want it. Washing is hung to dry on a line stretching from bow to stern. Sometimes you see a playpen on board, with one or two babies in it. Almost every barge has its dog acting as permanent officer of the watch.

A barge in a hurry can be a fearsome thing, bearing down in the centre of the channel if it is laden and needing the deepest water available. There is a tendency for the helmsman of a small boat to be drawn towards the mammoth vessel, like a rabbit mesmerised by a snake, because of the 'pull' of the water drawn by the barge. As long as you are aware of it, you can easily correct it. There is room for barges and pleasure craft to co-exist amicably.

Belgium has fewer lift bridges than Holland, but it has more lumps than its northern neighbour, so there are correspondingly more locks. These are staffed almost universally by pleasant, chatty fellows who deal swiftly with the minimal paperwork. The locks are closed on Sundays.

It is advisable to stock up with supplies when you stop at a town mooring because of those long stretches where there is no chance of buying so much as a kilo of Brussels sprouts. You sometimes find a shop near a lock.

The Belgian waterways present some lovely visual experiences: neat rows of trees perfectly reflected in unruffled water; a graceful bridge with a happy family of cyclists pausing to wave at you; red-roofed farm outbuildings with donkeys browsing and chickens scratching; early morning mist giving the promise of a sunny day ahead. The country has a great deal to offer the boating fraternity. A little effort and expenditure could lead to enormous improvements and upgrade the inland waterways to a major tourist attraction.

Getting Around

Holiday skippers are unlikely to be attracted to those canals carrying a lot of international commercial traffic – like the major route between Antwerp and Brussels – and they will probably be relieved to learn that in some cases, at least, it is possible to plan routes to avoid them.

Charts tend to be less detailed – and sometimes less accurate – than those in France and Holland. It's wise to check routes with the boat rental company, and to pick the brains of other boaters at locks and moorings.

Use of the Belgian waterways costs very little. The first lock keeper you encounter will want to see your boat's official papers and will ask where you are going before issuing a carnet which has to be presented at each lock office. The carnet is for a one-way trip. You pay the same fee (about 50 pence when we last cruised there) whether you plan to travel to the next lock or from one end of Belgium to the other. For the sake of bureaucracy, and to give yourself some leeway, the trick is to state a route a bit longer than you are actually considering because when you reach the last lock on the carnet, or turn round to go back, you'll have to pay another fee.

Pioneer Companies

Belgium's pioneer rental companies have set a high standard of boat and equipment. Green Waterway Holidays, operating its fleet from a quiet basin in the centre of Ghent, has quality crockery, glassware and bed linen, and the sleek and sturdy 36 ft (11 m) Pedro boats, built in Holland and powered by Volvo Penta diesel engines, can accommodate eight. With four on board in two double cabins, the comfort is superb. There is a refrigerator, shower, central heating and plenty of cupboard space.

The Pedro is a sea-going craft with such navigational niceties as depth sounder, speed gauge and bow thrusters – a boon when manoeuvring in confined spaces. The vessel has two steering positions – from the stern deck or amidships in the saloon, where the impressive instrument panel includes a stereo audio system.

Operating from Montigny near Charleroi on the River Sambre in the south of Belgium, Locaboat Plaisance offers a choice of *pénichettes*, with traditional high-bowed hull and five or seven berths, or cruisers accommodating up to four adults and two children. The Meuse Valley, a popular holiday region is within a few days' cruising of the base.

Visitors staying less than two months do not need a permit for cruising in Belgium, and now that boat rental facilities have been introduced, the country's two major regions at least can be explored by many more enthusiasts from abroad. The Flemish-speaking Belgians are mainly in the north-west, and the Walloons, or French-speaking inhabitants, are in the south. The cut-off line is distinct. If you need aspirins at Oudenaarde you get them from an *apotheek*. At nearby Tournai you look for a *pharmacie*.

Progressive Ghent

Ghent, capital of the province of East Flanders, is a busy inland port at the confluence of the Leie (in France it's the Lys) and the Schelde. The city has recently acknowledged the increasing interest in pleasure boating and yachting, and a long jetty has been built, turning a central waterway, unused by commercial carriers, into a marina and yacht club.

Ghent has about a quarter of a million people whose chief preoccupation, it may seem on a summer's day, is sitting in the open air

Typical scenery, Schelde

enjoying a glass of beer, the national drink. It wouldn't be a bad idea to join them while you get your bearings and decide what you want to see.

The city has many ancient and historic buildings, but little attempt is made to exploit them. They are part of everyday life, like the cobbled paths and streets. Ghent Tourist Office is in the crypt of the early-sixteenth-century town hall. You can take tours on foot, by boat or by horse and carriage. In the summer trip boats go to Bruges.

There is no shortage of places to eat – taverns, brasseries, restaurants, carveries, snack bars, grills, chip shops, cafés, and the ubiquitous 'fast food outlets'. The Belgians love their food rich and in quantity, and it would be a pity not to try some local specialities. There's *waterzooi* – fish boiled with herbs to make a soup; rabbit with prunes; hotchpotch, a stew made with poultry; mutton ragout; jugged hare. Green eel is a popular dish. The baby eels are cooked with mixed herbs – mint, verbena, parsley and sage – and the *anguilles au vert* can be eaten hot or cold.

Ghent is encircled by the **Ringvaart**, a sort of waterways M25 offering a choice of routes to all parts of the country – indeed, all parts of Western Europe. A quiet, narrow canal leads to it from the new moorings in the city centre.

Bruges – City of Bridges

To reach Bruges from Ghent, take the Ostend Canal. Predictably, perhaps, they call Bruges the Venice of the North. The name means bridges – there are about fifty of them – and a network of small canals and a wealth of old, gabled frontages contribute to the town's relaxed charm.

Capital of West Flanders province, Bruges is said to be the best preserved medieval city in Europe. An evening tour can be taken by trip boat on the city canals. Boat trips also go to Damme, an attractive little town north-east of Bruges. It takes about an hour each way.

There are more than 150 historic monuments in Bruges. To learn about a selection of them, take a guided city walk or a horse-drawn cab. Or you can go by minibus, with commentaries in a choice of seven languages relayed through headphones. In July and August, afternoon guided tours of the De Gouden Boom Brewery are given, complete with beer tasting. Flea markets are held on Saturdays and Sunday afternoons from May to October. There is a lace museum, with demonstrations of lace-making and items for sale.

Voyage to Ypres

To visit Ypres and the military cemeteries of World War I, go west to Niewport then left through Dixmude on the River Yser, and on to the Canal de l'Yser. The waterway halts at Ypres.

Known as 'Wipers' to the Tommies of World War I, Ypres has been largely rebuilt. The Menin Gate, a memorial to the quarter of a million British soldiers who died, bears the names of nearly 55,000 with no known graves. Buglers still sound the Last Post at 8 pm each day.

The first Sunday in May sees the Pageant of the Cats, with hundreds of participants enacting cat worship through the centuries. At the climax of the ceremony cats made of velvet or wood are thrown to the ground from high up in the town belfry, to drive away evil spirits. The custom echoes medieval times when cats were vital to exterminate the mice that invaded the Cloth Hall. When the annual cloth sales were over and the storage space cleared, the unfortunate cats, no longer needed, were flung to their deaths.

Through the Ardennes

With no way forward beyond Ypres, it's back to Bruges and Ghent to head towards Tournai via the Boven-Schelde. This takes you through **Oudenaarde**, known for its art and architecture, its Gothic town hall, its tapestries – and its summer beer festivals. The town is regarded as the gateway to the Flemish Ardennes.

Oudenaarde has good moorings, handy for the town centre, though you need to be a bit athletic to climb the steel ladders and over the railings at the edge of the cobbled quayside. There is a lift bridge across the waterway. Just give a long toot, and a cheery wave as you pass the bridge keepers' lodge. They're a jolly crowd.

At the next port of call, **Tournai**, on the Haut-Escaut Canal, you'll realise by listening to the townspeople, that you have reached French-speaking Belgium. The town has an impressive entry through a three-arched bridge flanked by round towers, the Pont-des-Trous, which was part of the defence system in the Middle Ages. Just beyond it are good moorings at the town quay. Again, though, you need to be agile.

Tournai's Cathedral of Notre Dame, with its five impressive towers, can be seen from many angles. Its construction began in 1110. There is also a Folklore Museum, a Museum of Fine Arts and a Museum of History and Archaeology.

The waterway divides after Tournai. Take the left fork and you enter the Nimy-Blaton-Peronnes Canal and head for **Mons**, with its bleak memories of two World Wars. The cemeteries are a short distance outside the town, and within it is a war museum – as well as several others.

Eastward from Mons, the Canal du Centre leads to **La Louvière** where hydraulic lifts – Houdeng-Goegnies and Houdeng-Aimeries – do the work of conventional locks, raising or lowering boats about 55 ft (16.5 m) to the next level. Built to the same design of Britain's Anderton Lift, in Cheshire, they were opened by King Leopold II in June 1888. Among those who celebrated the lifts' centenary in 1988 was a group from the UK Inland Waterways Association who had taken their boats to Belgium for the occasion.

At **Charleroi**, the Canal du Centre reaches a junction with the River Sambre. Charleroi, the biggest city in French-speaking Wallonia, is a big industrial centre. The Sambre here is a workaday river with wharves and cranes lining the banks.

River Meuse

The Meuse rises in France, flows through Belgium and reaches the sea as the Maas in the Netherlands after joining forces with the Waal. By the time it joins the Sambre at Namur it meanders through increasingly glorious scenery that is worth seeing from above. See if you can spot your moored boat as you take a cable car ride 400 ft (120 m) above the valleys of the Meuse and the Sambre.

This lovely region forms part of the Eastern Ardennes. Its high cliffs are topped with forest. Guided tours of some of the castles in the area are available in summer. People go hiking, cycling, canoeing and horse riding, and trip boats add to the holiday atmosphere.

Liège has been a coal-mining centre since the twelfth century, and barges laden with coal still ply the Meuse and the Albert Canal, which links the city with Antwerp. Sunday mornings in Liège see a very lively market on the banks of the Meuse.

As Wallonia's main cultural city, Liège has some splendid architecture, including the eleventh-century Bishop's Palace, now law courts. Each of the sixty columns surrounding the courtyard is different. For a large city, though, Liège has few night spots. Families and friends tend to get together round the table in the evenings.

From Liège you can continue north, close to the Dutch border, and complete a circuit to Ghent via the Albert Canal to Antwerp and the Zeeschelde via Dendermonde, but this would hardly be relaxed holiday cruising.

If you have cruised from Tournai to Liège without seeing **Dinant**, a town on the Meuse, due south of Namur, try to make a detour on the way back. Plan for an overnight stay. The river paints a picture of peace and prosperity, with the gardens of villas and wilder reaches edged with foxgloves and dog roses. But Dinant has had a turbulent history, including dreadful suffering in World War I. The surrounding area is peppered with castles.

Don't miss a guided tour of the grotto at nearby **Han-sur-Lesse**. The River Lesse has overhanging rocks, some shaped like animals, and there are nearby caverns, one with a stream flowing through it. But the grotto is the *pièce de résistance*. Visitors are led through tunnels, past weird rock formations into vast caves. One of them, The Dome, is more than 650 ft (195 m) high, another has a stalagmite with a radius of 60 ft (18 m) at its base.

The Lesse runs underground for a while. Boats are boarded in The Dome and passengers are carried through the darkness, peering at clusters of bats picked out by torchlight.

River Leie

Those with little time to spare might like to try a short cruise along the River Leie from Ghent to **Menin**, the last town in Belgium along this route before the border with France. It's a trip of about 47 miles (75 km), and although it passes through some fairly bleak agricultural land, the waterway takes in **Deinze**, one of the oldest towns in Flanders, and **Courtrai**, once the world centre of the flax industry. Courtrai has moorings in a backwater overlooked by the impressive fifteenth-century Broel Towers guarding each side of a bridge.

The Dendre

Another river accessible from either Ghent or Montigny is the Dendre, a smaller waterway than those already covered. It is fairly heavily locked but goes through a number of towns and villages. **Dendermonde** was badly knocked about in World War I and lost many of its historic monuments. But the Church of Onze Lième Vrouw has retained its treasures, including two Van Dycks, and an early Romanesque font. Aalst, capital of the Dendre country, is the centre of a hop-growing area. Its beer is renowned.

It's worth taking a stroll ashore at **Ninove** to see the fourteenth-century Town Gate, and at **Geraardsbergen** where there is a copy of the Mannekin Pis fountain donated by the city of Brussels. Another place to moor up is **Ath**, especially on the last Sunday in August when there is a parade of eight brightly coloured giants made of reeds. Three of them represent Goliath, his bride and Samson.

The River Dendre joins the Nimy-Blaton-Peronnes Canal just after Blaton.

Reaching Antwerp and Brussels means sharing the waterways with some of the biggest of the big boys. The canals are wide and deep, and with 3,500-tonne neighbours rushing about, – to say nothing of the lack of decent scenery – these are hardly the best waterways for pleasure craft.

Antwerp

Belgium's second largest city and the world's fifth largest port, Antwerp has nearly 60 miles (96 km) of quays and 40 sq. miles (64 sq. km) of harbour and docks. It has been an important diamond-cutting centre for 500 years, and the local tourist office can arrange for visitors to see cutters at work.

Antwerp has a strong cultural side. The cathedral, dating from 1352, has much to see, including three of Rubens's works. The artist's home can also be visited. The Steen, which goes back to the tenth century, contains the city's Maritime Museum.

A route from Antwerp to Brussels starts on the tidal reaches of the River Schelde. The first place of any size is **Hoboken**. The name means 'tall beeches', and there are a good many of them around, but Hoboken is a highly industrialised shipyard town. Next place to head for is **Rupelmonde**, and some careful navigation is called for after you've entered the tidal River Rupel, for several waterways converge in the area. You'll be looking for the Canal de Bruxelles. More industry, a bit of agriculture and the towns of Tisselt and Vilvoorde glide by – then the capital of Europe comes suddenly into view.

Brussels

Everyone goes to see the Mannekin Pis statue, just off the Grand Place. His precise history is unknown. On special occasions he is dressed in a suit. His wardrobe is extensive and includes clothing donated by British and American services after World War II. But Brussels is more than a tiny statue in a corner of one of the finest squares in Europe. It is a sophisticated international city with a constant traffic of statesmen, politicians, financiers, and media people attracted by the twin magnets of the NATO and EEC headquarters.

The city has lots of things to see, and there are many sightseeing tours. One attraction you can visit under your own steam is St Martin's Basilica at Halle, 10 miles (16 km) south-west of the capital, on the Canal Charleroi-Brussels. The Basilica has a statue of the Black Virgin, believed to perform miracles, and the town has been a place of pilgrimage since the thirteenth century.

Waterways Pilgrimage

The Canal Charleroi-Brussels draws pilgrims of a different kind: waterways enthusiasts. The canal underwent extensive modernisation in the 1960s, and at **Ronquières**, south of the village of Lembeek, is the stupendous inclined plane on which vessels up to 1,350 tonnes are carried up or down a one-in-twenty slope for more than three-quarters of a mile (1.2 km). The journey is made in a gigantic water tank on wheels, running on steel tracks. Operations are controlled from a 300 ft (90 m) tower and closed-circuit TV is used. Skippers are instructed by red and green signal lights and an amplified voice from the tower.

The Belgians are rightly proud of the Ronquières sloping lock, for in building it they led the world in modern canal engineering. They have even turned it into a tourist attraction. Visitors are able to see it in operation, watching from an eleven-storey-high public viewing platform. Spurred by the efforts of those pioneer companies at Bruges and Montigny, perhaps the Belgian authorities will soon view the whole canal system in the same light.

Addresses

General information

Belgian Tourist Office,
Premier House,
2 Gayton Road,
Harrow,
Middlesex HA1 2XU
Tel: 01-861 3300

Brochures/reservations

Andrew Brock Travel Ltd (UK agents for Locaboat Plaisance)
10 Barley Mow Passage,
London W4 4PH
Tel: 01-995 3642

Green Waterway Holidays,
5 Oud Strijderslaan
B8200 Bruges,
Belgium

STOP LOCK: THE PIONEERS

Kathleen Dugardyn, Belgian 'pioneer'

It was a dream – literally a dream while asleep – that led to the establishment of Green Waterway Holidays, a company in Belgium with a fleet of upmarket hire cruisers. Vincent and Kathy Dugardyn, in their thirties and living in Bruges, launched the Ghent-based business in 1988 with four beautifully fitted out steel-hulled Pedro 36 vessels, made in Holland, adding a Pedro 30 the following year.

'We were looking for a strong cruiser, easy to maintain and repair,' says Vincent. 'We think steel was, and still is, the best. After consulting the market, we found that Pedro gave us the best quality/price ratio compared to other steel boats.'

It was Vincent who dreamed that he had a boat-hire business on the Belgian canal system. When he awoke he thought it was a good idea and discussed it with his wife. Neither of them had any experience of inland boating. Both had sailed since childhood, and Kathy became an instructor with the Royal Belgian Sailing Club. They had been coastal cruising around the Channel Islands, Belgium, France and the United Kingdom.

The couple felt the Belgian canals, kept in good state by barge traffic from France, Germany, Holland and Belgium, had potential for leisure cruising. As it happened, someone else had similar thoughts and Belgium's first two inland cruiser hire fleets – the Dugardyns' and another in the south – started up in the same season.

Vincent, an insurance broker, had some capital to invest in a business, but was undecided about what type of business. His dream provided the answer. Kathy, a teacher of physical education and biology, did some research and gave up her job to get the company moving. Although recognising that Belgians are not natural sailors, she and Vincent believed there was a market among the French, British, Dutch and German peoples – in fact, Belgians made up the biggest number of their clients in the first year, followed by the Germans and the British.

Ghent Yacht Club and the local authority were extending the boardwalk jetties in that first season of the Green Waterway Holidays enterprise. But little else has been achieved in developing the tourism structure of Belgian waterways. Better signposting of canals, moorings between towns – virtually non-existent at present, except for the huge barges – and information about shops, restaurants, bars and places of interest within walking or cycling distance of the waterways – each Green Waterway vessel is equipped with bicycles – are needed. Facilities for pumping-out, refuelling and taking on water are almost non-existent.

The Dugardyns know what is required. Persuading the government that the waterways could work for Belgian tourism is another matter.

Kathy explains: 'There are a lot of possibilities in Belgium. The countryside is nice and typical. For people who want to see museums there is a big choice. But we don't get much response from the tourist offices. We have to promote Belgium as well as our firm, and the Ministry of Waterways still considers canals only as a necessity for professional inland shipping, and not for tourism. We would like to change that, but it is not easy. In Belgium there is the difficulty that the country has been federalised, so all the ministries have to split up into independent parts.'

It is easy to pass the buck.

'You contact one person who sends you to another,' says Kathy. 'Nobody wants to take any initiatives, and they pretend there is no money for improvements on the waterways – not for tourism, anyway.'

Nevertheless, Vincent and Kathy, who enjoy cruising their local canals with their young daughter and their dog, have plans for continued expansion. They have faith in the holiday product they offer. They attend international boat shows and travel trade conventions.

What has been the public reaction to the formation of Green Waterway Holidays?

'A lot of people find that we had a very good idea. Some find us eccentric. Some think we are mad! But a lot of people accept the idea of this form of tourism and intend to give it a try some time.'

TRAVEL
BOOKS
FROM

ASHFORD

UNDER MOUNT IDA

Reflections of Crete

Oliver Burch

A refreshing and original look at this most popular and historic of Mediterranean islands. Oliver Burch skilfully evokes the full character of both people and place, from the bleached hillside villages to the sun-drenched tourist beaches.
Tales from Crete's turbulent past combine with sometimes hilarious, sometimes sad encounters with the less-noble present to produce a fascinating portrait of this beautiful island under siege.

Hardback 288 pages   1 85253 202 5   £13.95

GROC's Candid Guides to
THE GREEK ISLANDS

Other titles in this series.

published by Ashford
1 Church Road, Shedfield, Hampshire, England. SO3 2HW

GROC'S Candid Guides to
THE GREEK ISLANDS

This highly acclaimed series has been continually refined to ensure that readers, be they armchair voyagers, annual holidaymakers or independent travellers, will be able to plunder a wealth of individualistic information, set out as a travelogue. The text is liberally interspersed with detailed maps and plans. As usual the guides praise the praiseworthy and damn the second rate.

The Cyclades Islands, Athens and Piraeus
2nd Edition
Geoffrey O'Connell
Fully updated including Syros, Mykonos, Paros, Naxos, Ios, Santorini, Amorgos Astipalaia, Tinos Andros, Sikinos, Folegandros, Milos, Siphnos, Serifos, Kithnos and Kea with excursion details to Delos, Antiparos, Anafi, Donoussa, Koufonissi, Shinoussa, Iraklia, Kimolos and Athens City, Piraeus and the mainland ports of Rafina and Lavrio.
Paperback 392 pages 56 maps and photographs   85253 174 6   £9.95

Crete, Athens and Piraeus
2nd Edition
Geoffrey O'Connell
Crete is not so much an island as a land in its own right. The guide has been divided into a number of regions based on individual cities and towns. The island and town maps are interspersed with pen and ink illustrations. The various routes are described in detail to facilitate holiday-makers' and travellers' exploration of this unique island.
Paperback 226 pages 19 maps and photographs   1 85253 090 1   £7.95

The Greek Mainland Islands
Geoffrey O'Connell
Including the Sporades and Argo-Saronic. Argo-Saronic include Salaminas, Aegina, Angistri, Poros, Hydra, Spetses and Kithira. Sporades include - Skyros, Alonissos, Skopelos, Skiathos and Evia.
Paperback 280 pages 30 maps and diagrams   1 85253 083 9   £8.95

Rhodes, The Dodecanese, Athens and Piraeus
Geoffrey O'Connell
Including Rhodes, Kos, Karpathos, Kasos, Simi, Tilos, Nisiros, Kalimnos, Leros, Patmos with excursion details to Chalki, Astipalaia, Kastellorizo, Pserimos, Yialos, Angathonisi, Arki and Lipsos.
Paperback 272 pages 31 maps and illustrations   1 85253 066 9   £8.95

Samos and the N.E. Aegean Islands, Athens and Piraeus
Geoffrey O'Connell
Including Samos, Ikaria, Fournoi, Thimena, Chios, Psara, Oinoussai, Lesbos, Limnos, Ag. Estratios, Thassos, and Samothraki as well as Athens City, Piraeus and the mainland ports of Kavala and Alexandroupoli.
Paperback 298 pages 36 maps and photographs   1 85253 898 9   £7.95

Please add 10 % p & p for orders by post

Enjoy a **real** holiday to the full!

The Alternative Holiday Guides provide all the relevant information and expert guidance required for your chosen holiday pursuit. The Guides look at specific activities rather than holiday centres and contain useful ideas for travel, tours, equipment, dos and don'ts and local information.